'S Wonderful!

About the Authors

Kevin Hough is a former producer/presenter with RTÉ Radio. Alison Maxwell is the author of *Jammet's of Dublin* and *Ronnie: The Authorised Biography of Veronica Dunne*.

'S Wonderful!
A Musical Life

Kevin Hough
with Alison Maxwell

The Liffey Press

Published by
The Liffey Press Ltd
'Clareville'
307 Clontarf Road
Dublin D03 PO46
www.theliffeypress.com

A catalogue record of this book is
available from the British Library.

ISBN 978-0-9957927-3-9

Printed in Ireland SprintPrint.

Contents

Chapter 1

Corned Beef and Cabbage, I Love You

It was the corned beef that nearly did me in.

Encased inside a fortress-like tin with a flimsy key to aid escape, Clover Meats took every care that the darned beef was almost impossible to extract. A customer's demand for a slice or two would strike terror into my heart, but I had devised a cunning plan. I would plunge the tin into hot water for a few seconds, then slot the key into the flap on the lid and peel back, give the whole lot a good shake and the beef would normally slide out. The one time it absolutely would not budge I got the bright idea of bashing it with a hammer, to no effect. The customer was waiting and I became hot with embarrassment as I wrestled with the wretched thing. Eventually I thrust a sharp knife up and around the inside of the tin and a somewhat mangled concoction plopped onto the counter. Phew!

Dad's shop on the Crumlin Road in the outskirts of Dublin was the kind of place you would find on the main street in every town in Ireland in the 1940s and '50s. It sold almost everything a housewife needed for the running of her home and family – bread, butter, milk, cheese, cooked meats, vegetables, biscuits, copybooks, pencils, sweets, even coal. Dad and Mam worked day and night at it, and the eight of us kids had to do our bit as soon as we were able. Even now, whenever I get a whiff of Brussels sprouts or the nose-crinkling reek of paraffin, it takes me back to those days in the shop.

My father, Michael Hough, was a country lad from County Limerick who had come to Dublin during the 1930s to work at Humphrey's Bar in Ranelagh. He was strong and athletic and at one time hurled for the Limerick GAA senior team. He was also smart – he did, after all, volunteer to train Éire Óg, the local ladies camogie team. It was there that he met the slim and pretty Patricia O'Rourke and her sister Maura and, although Maura was the better player, he pulled rank and appointed Patricia as the captain. Michael and Patricia discovered they shared a *grá* for music and performing and their friendship blossomed into a romance. Dad did not want to run a pub – he had seen the unhappiness inflicted on families when someone has a drink problem. On the other hand, everyone needed food, so he decided to go into the grocery trade. My parents married in 1936. They bought the shop in Crumlin with financial help from his parents, and moved into living quarters upstairs.

Three years later my sister Maura was born, then Ursula and Patricia. I arrived in 1944, and then there was another son who died when I was two. With the birth of my sister Fionnuala a couple of years later, we all moved into a large three-storey house in Beechwood Avenue, Ranelagh, which was owned by my grandmother, Mam's mother. That is where Philomena (Phil), Maeve and my brother Michael were born.

Wedding day of Patricia and Michael Hough, with
Patricia's parents (from left: Michael, Ellen O'Rourke,
Patricia, John O'Rourke, 1936)

With all those children, it was a blessing when Gran gave
Mam an electric washing machine. Gran and my Aunt Joan
lived in Kilmacud, about five miles away from us. Gran was
a real lady, and very generous, but she took her parenting
duties seriously. With my parents in the shop so much, Gran
would come over to our house and she could be quite stern,
but she cooked the best chips in the world.

Mam had to be wife, mother, housewife, shopkeeper
and accountant, but it didn't seem to faze her at all, and she
was really popular with the customers. We had a daily maid,
Mary, who tidied the house and cooked our midday meal.
Mary, God love her, was not gifted in the culinary department, but her dinners at least filled us up. Mam, on the other

hand, was a terrific cook, and we all learned by watching her and copying what she did.

At weekends and on our holidays and free afternoons, we went over to work in the shop. It was the proving ground for all of us, although some of the girls were not that keen. Dad looked after all the hauling, selling and buying, and he grew vegetables in the big garden behind the shop. Early in the morning, six days a week, he cycled the three miles into Dublin city to the Victorian red brick buildings that housed the Corporation Fruit and Vegetable Market on Mary's Lane. He ordered the day's supplies and would put as much as he could in his baskets before the long cycle back. As soon as he reached the canal bridge at Dolphin's Barn, he knew he was in for a slow hill climb up the Crumlin Road before the shop. The rest of the produce was delivered a couple of hours later by van, but Dad wanted to make sure that when he opened the shop there would be a display of fresh vegetables in the boxes outside the door. We were expected to help out by shifting crates, stacking shelves, dealing with customers, weighing provisions, handling money, cleaning up and taking orders. I was provided with a messenger bike, baskets front and back, and learnt how to balance briquettes, coal and groceries so as not to come a cropper.

The day our first car appeared outside the door we kids jostled each other in our excitement to take a look. It was a gleaming red Ford Estate. Dad tried to point out that the back seats could be folded down so that he could collect goods from the wholesalers, but all we wanted to know was could we go for a drive. He laughed and in we all piled. When we stopped at the traffic lights, we could see people's eyes popping in astonishment at the sight of Dad and Mam in the front, and one, two, three, four, five, six, seven, *eight* squirming heads in the back!

So long as the weather was fine the car started up like a dream, but it could be a different story early on a cold winter morning. My bedroom was in the front of the house and I would hear the front door open and close, then the bang of the car door and I would say a silent prayer that the next sound would be the engine kicking into life. As often as not, it would not, and I would have to get up and go out to push the car down the road. Bed never felt as warm and inviting as on those mornings when, after Dad had gone, I got that extra hour between the sheets before it was time for school. On Saturdays and school holidays I went with him to the market and to Fanning's Wholesalers in Cuffe Street and Fagan's near Liffey Street. He exchanged great banter with the traders and could give as good as he got, all at the crack of dawn. They looked after him well, but then, he was a good customer, always very particular about paying his bills on time.

My parents were scrupulous about keeping accounts, but once a year my mother got extremely nervous when she had to face the taxman. She was normally very careful with her appearance, but for that particular visit she always wore an old threadbare coat in the hope that he would go easy on her. Their bank account was with the local Munster and Leinster Bank, and they must have been valued because every Christmas the manager would send us a tin of sweets and a box of biscuits, which was a bit like sending coals to Newcastle, but the thought was appreciated. Dad also gave out Christmas presents but as the family grew larger and money became tight, that had to stop, but his regulars remained loyal. He

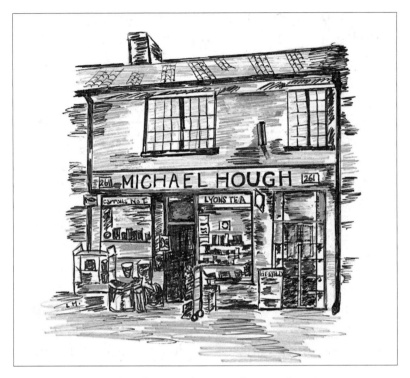

Hough's Shop on the Crumlin Road, 1950
(Drawing by Lucinda Maxwell)

was known throughout the district as being fair and honest, a decent man, which was the highest praise.

The 1940s and '50s were hard times and people could easily run short of money before the week was out. Dad did not like to see anyone go cold or hungry and he often extended too much credit. A lot of customers had weekly accounts, and after we served them, we would make out a docket and stick it on a skewer. These details were entered into a ledger every evening by Mam and totted up at the end of the week. I used to dread Saturday afternoons when I had to go around the houses with the bills, each carefully written out and put in an envelope. Most people paid on time, but some ran up big amounts and then did their best to avoid paying anything. When they saw me coming they pretended not to be in, but I could see them peeping from behind the curtains. Others would be just plain abusive and it was a struggle to even get two shillings off them. It was a tough job, but at least I had a good meal and a warm fire to look forward to when I got home, not like some. I will always remember one bitter winter's day when a young girl in ragged clothes came into the shop. After she left, my father said, 'God love her, Kev. She hasn't enough on her that would wipe a knife.'

As soon as the newspapers arrived in the morning they were stacked on the counter. I remember one of the headlines in big bold lettering announcing that the Abbey Theatre had been destroyed by fire; that was in July 1951. In January 1952, another shocking story was of the first fatal crash of an Aer Lingus plane. The 23 passengers and crew were killed when it plunged into a mountain in Snowdonia, Wales during a blinding rainstorm.

All the papers to be delivered had to be marked up. Even now, those names and addresses are ingrained on my brain because I had to know where each of the customers lived. To this day if someone mentions, say, Mrs Bob O'Connor, I immediately think of 4 Curlew Road and the route on my bike. The man who lived at 20 Iveagh Gardens was tall and had a terrible smoker's cough and I was afraid of him because he was so grumpy. Nearly everyone bought a newspaper and we stocked the *Irish Press*, *Irish Independent*, the *Herald* and the *Evening Mail*, and the *Sunday Press* and *Sunday Independent*. One lady always put on her gloves when collecting her paper because she did not want the print on her hands. It got onto our hands, alright, and we would have to wash them before handling cold meats or strings of sausages.

Very few foodstuffs came ready-packed, so we weighed what we could before the shop opened in the morning and after it closed at night. Lyons tea was pre-packed, but loose Mazawattee tea was delivered in wooden chests, and when the lid was prised off I would wonder if faraway Ceylon smelt as dusky and warm. That tea was stored in a great bin at the back of the shop, and every day it was weighed out on the Avery scales, scooped into brown paper bags and sealed with a special fold to be sold at one and sixpence a quarter pound. Jam-making season was always a busy time in the sugar department. Loose sugar came in a hessian sack that had to be raised on wooden boards to keep it dry off the floor, and we sold it in one-pound, two-pound and sometimes seven-pound bags. Butter was delivered in specially sloped boxes so it was easy to dislodge onto the counter where we shaped it into one pound blocks using wooden paddles. It glistened thick and yellowy, and beads of moisture formed on the top as we wrapped it in greaseproof paper to store in the fridge. When we got supplies of rabbits, my father would skin them on the same counter, using lots of newspaper of course, but the myxomatosis disease pretty well finished them off. Bottles of milk were fresh every day, and customers used the cream off the top for desserts.

The complicated system of Imperial weights and measures came as second nature to us: 16 drams to an ounce; 16 ounces to a pound; 7 pounds to a clove; 14 pounds to a stone; 2 stones to a quarter; 4 stones to a hundredweight – oh, I could do it in my sleep. People might want a couple of ounces of this or a quarter-pound of that and I had to learn to make rapid price calculations in pounds, shillings and pence. In the early days, money was kept in a wooden drawer with different compartments for farthings, ha'pennies, pennies, thrupences, sixpences, shillings, two shillings and half-crowns. The section for ten shilling and pound notes saw precious little use. Later on, we got a cash register, but I have never lost the ability to do quick tots in my head.

How I hated Wednesdays and Fridays – fish days! Morton's of Ranelagh delivered it fresh on large tin trays filled with ice, but it stank the place out. Those were the days when I loved getting out on my bike to deliver the papers or anything else, but when I came back the fish would still be there. Ray, plaice, sole, cod, haddock, herrings, mackerel and whiting (some people called it 'whitening'), but ray was the very worst. It was slimy and slippery to pick up and prone to slithering away. Herrings were nearly as bad with their scales that would stick to my hands and get under my nails. The fish was placed on greaseproof paper, weighed and then wrapped in newspaper. After that, there was nothing for it but to wash my hands in the kitchen at the back of the shop, probably keeping a customer waiting who wanted a few ounces of cheese. Then, get the block of cheese on the red slicing machine with its circular razor-shape blade, cut it, weigh it, wrap it, write out the docket and attend to the next person who might be looking for a quarter stone of potatoes.

The vegetables – potatoes, cauliflowers, cabbages, carrots, turnips, lettuce –were stacked outside next to a weighing scales on a crate, and every day we wrote out prices on the window pane above. Sometimes Dad boiled several varieties of potatoes to demonstrate to people how they differed. Golden Wonders were popular but tricky to cook because they were floury and could turn to mush very quickly. Queen's were a good all-rounder and sold well. Some canny customers picked all the big ones out of the sack leaving the tiddlers behind, which caused no end of annoyance. In wet weather I got mucky from weighing the spuds so it was back to the kitchen again to wash. In, out, in, out, forty times a day, and that was before we had to go to the shed at the back of the shop for coal, logs and briquettes, or to measure a quart of paraffin into someone's container.

At midday we closed for an hour for our dinner and the vegetables had to be taken in. Invariably we would hear the ring of the phone in the public telephone box on the street; we always ran to answer it because it could be an order. It might be Mrs Nutty from Raphoe Road wanting half a block of HB ice cream from our freezer for her husband's dessert, and I would have to put off my dinner and speed down to the Nuttys on the bike before the ice cream melted. Daddy called it customer service, but I called it something else entirely.

When people came in for a wafer, I used the marker that was kept in a jar of water to measure the tuppeny, thrupenny, fourpenny or sixpenny ice cream they wanted. The sixpenny was a whopper – you could hardly get your jaw around it. Choc ices were easier, straight from the freezer, and we made our own ice-pops for next to nothing out of cordial and water and sold them at a penny each.

Fresh bread was delivered every day by van. The large wooden trays it came on were useful for covering the bare concrete floor behind the counter. But our feet and legs ached from standing all day, and the only thing after work was a good soak in a basin of hot water and Radox. In winter, the cold in the shop seemed to penetrate every bone, and then my weekly bath with lashings of Radox on a Saturday night was a great comfort. With the eight of us, we had to negotiate when and for how long we could use the bathroom, which often caused ructions, especially with all those girls.

Hot weather brought its own challenges in the shop – *bluebottles*, buzz, buzz, buzzing around the fish, the meats, the fruit. Dad hung up sticky flypapers and it was one of my jobs to take them down, full of dead and dying flies and wasps – ugh! The fly spray, on the other hand, was a grand weapon that I used liberally and with enthusiasm, but Dad curtailed this activity on the grounds that the sides of bacon might get poisoned.

Eggs, cheap and nutritious, were always in demand. A man from Monaghan supplied them and they were the freshest you could get. Someone might come in asking for just one egg and two ounces of cheese cut thinly. Afterwards, Dad would shake his head sadly and say, 'It would be a mean mouse that would eat that.'

Dad trained many assistants in the shop. One of them was John O'Byrne from Iveagh Gardens, Crumlin. John later managed Dobbin's Bistro, the famous Dublin restaurant. When any of our family dined at Dobbin's, John always made a point of telling other customers that he had learned his trade from my father.

It was good fun when the shop was busy. If someone was in a hurry, other customers generally didn't mind giving up their turn because they could have a chat with their neighbours. But it was a seven-day-a-week job and Sunday afternoons could drag. I used to bring a transistor radio with me and tune into the BBC Home Service (I preferred Radio Luxembourg but that did not start until six o'clock, and anyhow it was impossible to get any sort of reception as long as there was daylight). *Sing Something Simple* was a great programme that featured the Mike Sammes Singers who harmonised to such old favourites as 'Moonlight and Roses', 'Louise', 'Leaning on a Lamppost', 'Little Annie Rooney', 'On Mother Kelly's Doorstep', 'Daisy Bell' and 'Auntie Maggie's Remedy'. I grew to love those songs and even to this day, without thinking too much, I can rattle them off on the piano and still remember the words.

Sunday was a popular day for the cinema, and dealers who had stalls in the city centre during the week would call into the shop for a few cigarettes on their way over to the Star Cinema to sell off the last of their sweets and fruit. The apples, especially, would be well past their best. On one occasion Dad remarked that they were going to have a hard job getting rid of them, but he was assured that, with a judicious rub from a bit of rouge, the apples would come up nice and rosy! I grew very fond of the dealers, and years later when I worked for Radio Éireann I got to know them even better as I walked along Moore Street.

The customers were the heart of the shop. Kids coming in for a pennyworth of sweets out of the tall glass jars, or being sent on 'messages' by their mother for that one egg and thinly sliced cheese. The elderly who carefully counted their pennies in an effort to eke out the pittance that was their old age pension. Or the men who called in on their way from work for a packet of Woodbine or Gold Flake, Sweet Afton or Players. But most of all there were the women. In the era before refrigerators and supermarkets, women shopped daily for their families, sometimes two or three times a day, in order to get the freshest bread, milk or meat. Their husbands came home at one o'clock for dinner, and, having been in earlier, a woman might pop back for a tin of peas or a head of cabbage or a few slices of Denny's ham if the weather was good. They had stories about everything and an answer for anything and we had many a laugh together, but with some of their serious comments it was all we could do to keep a straight face. I remember Dad enquiring after one man who hadn't been in for his paper for a few days and his wife saying his 'various' veins were giving him a bit of trouble.

The church was just up the road, and before weddings we did a good trade in confetti at fourpence halfpenny a box. It was kept on one of the highest shelves out of the way. One day a woman came in and asked for a packet. I duly got out the ladder, climbed to the top shelf, fetched a box, came down and handed it to her. 'What's this?' she asked. 'I don't want confetti for a weddin', I want it for the soup!' Soup mix, a colourful assortment of dried peas, lentils and barley – what else would it be called but confetti?

Another time a woman asked me for some 'boddery biscuits'. Though I was familiar with most things in the shop, I had never heard of that brand. I wracked my brain to think what they might be.

'Would they be Bourbon biscuits?' I asked in my best secondary school accent.

'No,' she said. 'You know the ones like fingers to stick in the tea and for the babby to suck?'

The penny dropped. 'Ah, of course,' I said, and handed over a packet of Boudoir biscuits.

We had a lot of Church of Ireland customers. One genteel lady came in every other day for a loaf of Procea bread and she would blanch at the bad language of another, particularly awkward, customer, let us call her Mrs Dunne. One day Mrs Dunne arrived trussed up in a stiff white collar. I asked Olive, one of the assistants, 'What happened to her? Did she have whiplash or something?'

Quick as a whippet, Olive replied, 'No, I think someone wrung her neck for her!'

There were always the customers who tried to pull a fast one. One woman would waylay the bread man for a loaf and tell him she would fix up with Mister Hough later. Dad was scrupulous about keeping records and would notice the missing loaf. When he asked for payment, the woman always feigned surprise, saying she had forgotten. Once, she nicked clothes from a neighbour's clothesline. The neighbour told me that a few days later that she saw the kids from next door walking down the road in her own children's clothes. Years later I realised that poverty drives people to do desperate things.

People thought there was only one way to get rich quick in the 1950s and that was through buying a lottery ticket with the Irish Hospitals' Sweepstake. Customers were talking about it in the shop one day and Dad asked one of them if she was lucky.

'Jaysus no, Mr Hough,' she said. 'I'm so unlucky, if it was rainin' soup I'd be left standin' with a fork.'

The doors of the shop closed at 8 o'clock every night, but that did not mean that the day's work was done – far from it. The vegetables had to be taken in and sorted, the premises swept and cleaned, the meat slicer dismantled and washed. The fridge had to be tidied, and shelves were restocked with popular items like Vosene shampoo, Saxa salt and packets of Persil and Surf washing powder. Tea, sugar, butter and other commodities had to be weighed and packaged. Account dockets were removed from the spike and details entered into the ledger. Supplies for the following day had to be assessed and ordered. Unsold newspapers were pierced at the corner and threaded with twine to be hung on the nail at the end of the counter to be used as wrapping.

When everything was done, we counted and bagged the money to take home, and then locked up as securely as we could. But we got burgled several times all the same. The thieves were after just one thing – cigarettes. It was a terrible shock for Dad to arrive in the morning and find the place ransacked. He would make hasty repairs to doors and windows, but still had to go to the market for fresh produce – he did not like to see his customers disappointed because of some ne'er-do-wells. It would be a bad day indeed if fresh vegetables were not outside the door of Hough's Shop on the Crumlin Road.

Chapter 2

Sounds of Music

You might think that with all the hard work my parents put in at the shop there would be little time for them to do anything else, but there was plenty of fun, particularly with my mother. She sang and played the piano for us when we were small. I remember a very dramatic piece about the sinking of the *Titanic*. The song began as the ship set sail from Belfast and had a merry section in the middle with people dancing on the deck. Then came a dreadfully loud and ominous part when the ship hit the iceberg – that always made me shiver – and it ended with 'Nearer My God to Thee'. I wish I had that sheet music now; talk about stirring the imagination!

I learnt a lot about interpretation from my mother. She could be melodramatic one moment, and then turn around and sing songs like 'Christopher Robin Is Saying His Prayers' in a sweet and plaintive voice. When time allowed, Mam didn't need too much persuading to go greyhound racing at Shelbourne Park with one of our regular customers, Mrs O'Connor, whose husband Bob worked on the tote. They both enjoyed a flutter and a good night out.

All eight Hough children at the seaside, 1953
(From left: Maura, Ursula, Patricia, Kevin, Fionnuala,
Phil, Maeve and baby Michael)

Mam always seemed to be in good form and was very sociable. She and her sisters, Joan and Maura, got together once a week in each other's houses for cut-throat games of cards or Scrabble, with lively chat and tea and cakes afterwards. It was a custom that continued all their lives. Their brothers, Pat and Sean, often joined them in our house for games of Twenty-Five, considered to be the national card game of Ireland.

In the summer, Mam might suddenly announce that she was bringing us all for a picnic. We would bustle around assembling sandwiches, hard-boiled eggs and bottles of lemonade and slabs of cake, and tear off to the railway station that was just around the corner for the jaunt out to the beach at Killiney, Shankill, Bray or Greystones. However we managed it, sand always wound up in the sandwiches and half the lemonade got spilled, and there would be squabbles about who was to blame, but that was all part of the adventure. On the tiring walk back from the beach to the station at Shankill, we usually stopped at a little shop for ice cream and lollies; nothing tasted so good after a long, hot day by the sea.

Several of Mam's poems were published in *Ireland's Own* and in national papers. Here's one she wrote about all of us after we had grown up:

Our Family

Our dear first-born was Maura for
whom we waited three long years,
And on that happy day in May,
there were many joyous tears.

Our second daughter Ursula was
as quiet as a mouse,
As soon as she got on her feet she
was tidying the house.

And then a third, Patricia came to
fill our home with joy,
Ma said ' name her after yourself
and the next will be a boy.'

So sure enough our son was born,
red-haired we called him Kevin,
And then another baby boy who
went straight back to Heaven.

Our fourth daughter Fionnuala
was the destructive one,
She spilled and broke, and wasted
our cosmetics, just for fun.

Next came dear Philomena with
blue eyes and blondy hair.
She was always a quiet one, and no
trouble to rear.

Then Maeve was born, also blonde
and blue-eyed like her sister,
When she grew up, the lure of for-
eign travel just possessed her.

But Kevin was to have a pal, once
more the stork did call.
And Michael blonde and blue-eyed
came, the last one of them all.

Five daughters now are married
and as happy as can be,
So the family that filled our home is
now reduced to three.

But all are very happy, no rows or
falling out,
This life is very short indeed, there's
enough trouble about.

I think of all the blessings that
around us we can see,
And there's nothing in the whole
wide world like
'A HAPPY FAMILY'

These really were her sentiments. She enjoyed each of us in our own ways, and while I do remember childish rows they were never serious. Well, until the day that one of my older sisters tried to kill me! When I was four I was given a tricycle for Christmas and this particular sister (who shall be nameless) convinced me to cycle it down the stairs. Luckily, a pedal caught in the banisters and I landed in a heap about six steps down. There was war with my parents and a gate was put on the stairs the next day.

My dad was a most unselfish man who gave everything to rear and educate his family, never expecting anything in return. We were lucky to spend so much time with him in the shop because he seldom got back to the house much before nine in the evening, and he worked most weekends. The one full day we could be sure about having him at home was Christmas Day. On the odd occasion that he took an afternoon off, he liked to bring Patricia and myself to a hurling match in Parnell Park. Dad always knew about everything that was happening to the eight of us. If we had exams or concerts or something important coming up, he made a point of paying a special visit to the church on James's Street on his way back to the shop from the markets. There, he would light a candle and say a prayer for us. It was a comforting thought.

During the week we children had our chores around the house, as well as at the shop. The older ones had to take care of the younger ones. There was always sweeping and cleaning to be done. We had four flights of stairs, so there was a lot of polishing as well – I would put heavy socks over my shoes to minimise the effort. Each evening we knelt to say the Rosary together. On Saturday nights we took it in turn to polish the shoes, make stuffing for the next day's chicken and set the jelly. On Sunday morning we went to Mass. On Sunday evenings we gathered with family and our friends the O'Sullivans for music sessions in our house or theirs. Everyone was expected to do his or her turn. Father Bob Kelly, one of my teachers in primary school, entertained us with Percy French songs. My mother had a repertoire of Irish songs, and we younger ones began introducing Sinatra numbers and hits from Hollywood movies. Dad and Gran (Mam's mother) sang and played the concertina, and Dad played the fiddle as well. We each learnt to play instruments, and to this day we all sing. Maura plays the cello. Ursula and Patricia are violinists and Fionnuala is the soprano. I am the piano player, Phil plays the violin, Maeve plays violin and cello and Michael is the drummer. At one time or another each of the Hough children has trouped through the doors of the Dublin College of Music, sometimes altogether.

The girls went to St Louis Convent School, Rathmines. It was, and still is, a great school for music and they all blossomed musically. Maura sang leading roles in musicals and was brilliant at comedy. She was a diligent big sister and would always keep an eye on us if Mam was busy in the shop. When I was small, I remember her telling me to wash my hands or I would get polio! Maura would think nothing of bringing three or four of us on the bus out to Dollymount Strand to paddle in the sea and home again for tea. She was the apple of Dad's eye. One afternoon when she was about sixteen she met up with a few guys in Cervi's, the chipper that was just three doors from our shop. Dad wasn't having that – he marched straight down and fetched her back. As Maura said, not a lot could happen in a few yards. A few years later she married and went to live in Navan, and I think Dad missed her a lot.

Ursula was very bright at school and talented on the stage, and a stunner to look at. The evening she went to her debs dance in the Shelbourne Hotel, my Aunt Joan, who was wardrobe mistress at the Gate Theatre, dressed her in a costume that could be seen nightly on stage in *The Lady of the Camellias*, and she was beautiful. I loved watching all the girls perform, and when Ursula joined the Rathmines and Rathgar Musical Society (the R&R) in 1958 to sing in *Oklahoma!*, I saw the show three times in two weeks. It was while singing with the R&R that Ursula met Frank Gormley, a tailor from Donegal. They were mad about each other and got married in 1961. Ursula was the first of the family to marry, and lived in Rathmines, quite near to us. She was a violinist with the RTÉ Concert Orchestra for years.

Patricia had a beautiful soprano voice and she worked hard at improving it, training with Maura Tyrrell and later with Veronica Dunne. She loved entering and winning competitions at the Feis, and performed at school and with the Clontarf Musical Society and the R&R. My mother's brother Pat O'Rourke cast her in lots of his musicals, and she was the principal girl in pantomime with the Jack Cruise Company at the Olympia Theatre, Dublin. Right up to the early 1980s Patricia was still winning singing competitions, notably at the Waterford International Festival of Music, and then she directed her years of expertise and experience into conducting the choir in Dundrum Church, Dublin.

Fionnuala was a magnificent soprano, destined for a career in opera. She sang and performed at school, and later trained with Veronica (Ronnie) Dunne at the College of Music. Fionnuala studied in Rome for three years with Maestro Calcatelli, who had also trained Ronnie. Following appearances with the R&R and at venues around the country, she toured as a soloist with the Aer Lingus Singers. Fionnuala sang with English National Opera North in the early 1980s before settling back in Ireland.

Phil (who at the age of six forbade us on pain of death to call her Philomena) was a regular performer at St Louis Convent School, and later joined the St Louis Past Pupils' Musical Society. She won awards at the Waterford Festival, and sang and played violin at the Jurys Cabaret in Dame Street. Nowadays, Phil sings with Our Lady's Choral Society. Phil attended school at the same time as Irene McCoubrey (later known as Maxi) and Adèle King (later known as Twink), and they all went on to sing with the renowned Young Dublin Singers.

The youngest daughter, Maeve, was referred to locally as 'The News of the World'. She knew everyone's business because the neighbours loved her so much they would tell her anything. She had long blonde hair and was so thin she looked as if you could blow her down in a breath. When she played her cello in the school orchestra, she almost disappeared behind it. She once sang the role of Pali in *The Gypsy Baron*. Unfortunately, she laughed in the middle of it and when she came off stage a nun slapped her hard across the face. Undeterred, Maeve has always been involved in singing groups at home and on her many sojourns abroad. As my mother said, foreign travel lured her out of Ireland many times, but not away from her musical ties. When she lived in The Gambia, one of Africa's smallest countries, Maeve sang as one of the three little maids with an Irish society that produced *The Mikado*. She lives a bit closer to home now, in Greystones, and is a member of a folk group.

After his first few years at St Louis Infant School, my brother Michael attended Synge Street Christian Brothers

School. He was a very good student and keen about technical things like Meccano that had to be built from scratch. Michael studied percussion with Joe Bonnie at the College of Music. His drumming took him all over Ireland playing in céilí bands, and he was a regular with the Nenagh Musical Society where he accompanied the pianist Albert Healy. Michael sang with the St Louis Past Pupils' Musical Society, and even learnt to dance in musicals directed by Alice Dalgarno. He always enjoyed working with my father, and he now has his own shop in Dunshaughlin, County Meath. Michael is big into his sports and is a keen golfer.

And where, you may well ask, is Kevin amongst all these amazingly multi-talented people? You could say that my introduction into education and music did not go smoothly – in neither did I shine. Like the others, I started off at St Louis Infants where I, too, met Maxi and Twink, little knowing that I would have so much to do with them in later life. Then I went to St Mary's Junior School in Rathmines, where they actually togged me out in rugby gear and thrust me onto the pitch. But at the age of nine my rugby career was dashed. Cycling home from school one day, I strung my boots over the handlebars. They got caught in the spokes; I went over the top and chipped one of my front teeth. While the injury had little to do with playing rugby, I used it as an excuse for an early retirement. Now, if anyone expresses surprise that I ever played rugby, I point to my tooth and say, 'How do you think I got this?'

Ursula was studying violin with Sheila O'Loughlin at the College of Music and winning prizes in the Feis Ceoils, so my mother thought I should follow suit. Every Saturday morning I was let off school early for music theory and violin lessons, but somehow I never got the hang of it and I switched to piano. That did not go much better. My teacher was a melancholy woman who, now that I look back on it, may have been in some sort of pain, and not only from my playing. During our half-hour sessions, I was mesmerised by her habit of chewing Anadin tablets that were lined up on top of the piano. I stuck it for two years before discovering that by the gift of God or nature, I had a good ear and could play tunes just by listening to them, so I chucked the lessons.

I was a shy child, protected by my sisters (usually). Patricia was closest to me in age, just two years older, and we got into many scrapes together. One of our favourite haunts was the Milltown Golf Club where we used to have picnics with small bottles of orange pop, sandwiches and sweets. Sometimes Patricia brought her doll's pram out and we went for walks in Palmerstown Park. We once found a hedgehog there, which seemed incredibly exotic, straight out of Beatrix Potter, and we scooped him into the pram and brought him home to Beechwood Avenue. Gran, who was fanatical about cleanliness, hit the roof crying, 'Fleas! Fleas!'

Another time, Patricia and I were allowed to go the Metropole Cinema in O'Connell Street to see *Peter Pan*. We enjoyed it so much we stayed on for the second screening, and by the time we got home it was dark. Gran met us at the door with a face of thunder and told us she had been just about to call the police.

I adored theatre and films and always got around my parents to let me go to matinées. Mam shared my love of movies and if she got home early from the shop we would go together, provided I had finished my homework. Our local cinema was the Sandford in Ranelagh, and it was there that my love affair with the silver screen began.

Patricia and I went to Saturday matinées, and from the second I walked through the cinema doors and saw the dazzling posters and bold exclamatory wording it was all pure excitement. There was *Tiger Woman* – the jungle queen who had amazing adventures like 'The Temple of Terror', 'The Dungeon of the Doomed' and 'Triumph Over Treachery'. We had to keep going back each Saturday for the next instalment. It was the same with the *Flash Gordon* series. We were always left with a cliff-hanger – a truck hurtling towards the edge of a ravine or the evil genius Ming the Merciless about to annihilate our hero Flash.

Not all cinemas were the same. On Sundays we went to the Stella in Rathmines. It was bigger than the Sandford and usually crowded with people who smoked so much that it was often difficult to see the screen through the fug, and when the lights came up the ceiling and walls were a smeary brown colour, but we didn't care. It was the golden era of musicals and I just lapped it up – *Singin' in the Rain, A Star is Born, The Student Prince, Has Anybody Seen My Gal?, Carmen Jones, Meet Me in St Louis.*

The Green Cinema on St Stephen's Green stank of Jeyes Fluid (I will leave it to your imagination as to why that was so). There, I was awestruck by Jane Wyman and Rock Hudson in *All That Heaven Allows* and *Magnificent Obsession*, and I saw *Porgy and Bess* with the fabulous music of George Gershwin, and *Can Can* with Frank Sinatra and Shirley MacLaine.

Some cinemas presented live variety shows between the first and second film. In the centre of Dublin, the Regal Cinema was attached to the Theatre Royal which had a dance troupe called The Royalettes, famed for the inspired choreography of Alice Dalgarno and Babs de Monte. Just two weeks after the Regal screened *Exodus* with Paul Newman and Eva Marie Saint, Alice Dalgano produced a spectacular number for her dancers and the Jimmy Campbell Singers with the entire company dressed as Israelites escaping from Egypt.

There were three cinemas we were not allowed to set foot in: the Star in Crumlin and the Prinner (Princess) in Rathmines because they drew a 'rough crowd', and the Tivvo (Tivoli) in Francis Street where you could gain admission with glass jam jars that were then a valuable commodity.

Like most kids in those days, Patricia and I were allowed to roam freely. Everyone, even children, smoked and we wanted to be the same as the kids we hung around with. We once cadged eightpence halfpenny from my father and bought five Woodbines from William Maher's shop on Dunville Avenue before we headed off to meet our friends under the railway bridge. The cigarettes were very crude and had no filter tips, and even then were referred to as 'coffin nails'. I wanted to be cool like the guys in the movies, inhaling and blowing the smoke out through my nose. Instead, I got hot tobacco on my lips and burning smoke down my throat and I thought I would choke to death! Neither Patricia nor myself have smoked since.

We children usually spent a few weeks every summer down in my father's home place, Monagea in County Limerick. The farm had been left to his brother John, and he and Aunt Bridgie and my cousins always made us welcome. For city kids it was a whole other world, and we were expected to muck in. Life on the farm, indoors and outdoors, was hard. Auntie Bridgie cooked amazing meals on her small turf range. Helen, her eldest daughter, was a great help. She thought nothing of killing a hen by putting it under her arm and twisting its neck. The bird would be hung to let the blood drain out, and then Helen would pluck it and gut it ready for the evening meal. All the vegetables were home-grown, and I collected apples from the orchard for my aunt to make steaming hot tarts.

In the kitchen was a big open fire of turf and logs; I was fascinated by the way the flames flared when I pumped the bellows. The fire was never let go out, and boiling water in the black kettle slung on an iron pothook was always at the ready to make tea when neighbours called by. There was electric light in the house, but no washing machine. Clothes were washed by hand in the nearby stream, using a large washboard that hung beside the hall door. There were no toilets. Chamber pots, kept under the beds, had to be emptied daily, usually by Helen.

In Dublin, if we wanted rashers and sausages we bought them in the shop. In Monagea they caught a pig, tied it to a table outside and slit its throat. To this day I can still hear the poor creature's screeches, but that was life and the pig was soon butchered and parcelled up and I went with my cousins to deliver pork to the neighbours. Hens scurried around the yard at the back door and some laid their eggs in bushes, so one of my jobs every morning was to go on an egg hunt. I loved feeding the calves, and I learned to milk cows by hand – squirt, squirt, squirt into the bucket and the froth foaming on top. Neighbours helped us to save the hay, turning and gathering and stacking into ricks, then we helped them.

Some evenings we went for a walk around the village. When we were young my cousin Liam took much delight in frightening the life out of us as we passed the graveyard by jumping out with a sheet over his head! His sisters, Helen and Mary-Ita, brought us to Latchford's Cinema in Newcastle West where we climbed to the good seats upstairs. Downstairs the seats were wooden form benches. Inevitably, some smart aleck would start rocking the benches until there was an almighty crash as everyone fell to the ground and the usher would have to rush in to sort things out, while we smugly watched the fun from the balcony.

Every Saturday night Helen polished the men's shoes so they would be spick and span for Sunday Mass. After Mass we visited my dad's other brother Bill and his wife Lena who lived in a posh house up the road from the farm. Shiny as my shoes might be, Auntie Lena always made me take them off before entering her house. Uncle Bill was the head teacher in Monagea School where Auntie Lena also taught. Uncle Bill, William 'Willie' Hough, was famous in the area for having won three Munster medals and two All-Ireland medals with the Limerick senior hurling team. After his retirement he took an active role in the administration of the Munster Council of the Gaelic Athletic Association. He was a most generous man, and at a time when money was tight he would slip a few bob into our hands before we left for Dublin, laden with soda bread baked by our lovely Auntie Bridgie.

My dad had two sisters, both nuns, and when they came to Monagea or to our house in Ranelagh a great fuss would be made of them. On the farm, Auntie Bridgie's daughters would be moved out of their bedrooms and have to sleep in one of the outhouses. When they visited us in Ranelagh, Dad never called his sisters by their given names but always formerly addressed them as 'Sister'. These aunts were determined that at least some of my sisters would join them in the convent – no chance – and I remember being very small and sitting on one of these aunts' knees when she said, 'Sure, isn't Kevin going to be a priest?'

Just then a train rattled over a nearby railway bridge. 'I don't want to be a priest,' I said. 'I want to be a train driver!'

My parents sometimes rented a summer house in Bray, County Wicklow or Skerries, County Dublin for a month. Dad would drop Mam and us there in the car and then try to come down whenever he could at the weekends. The seaside resort of Bray was popular with lots of Dublin people. I loved the smell of fish and chips drenched in salt and vinegar in hot, greasy bags, and my pocket money would dwindle very quickly at Dawson's Amusement Arcade.

Skerries in the summer was notable for its 'fit-ups', travelling theatre groups that travelled from town to town, erected a tent and put on melodramas and musicals for a few days. These shows occasionally featured the stocking-clad legs of comely dancing girls and salacious themes from French farce, and were roundly condemned by local priests from the altar as being 'wicked and sinful'. When that happened, it ensured a sell-out crowd! The fit-ups were an old theatrical tradition in which many fine actors such as Anew McMaster, Cyril Cusack, Anna Manahan and Milo O'Shea cut their teeth; sadly the fit-ups disappeared in the late 1960s. I will never forget Vic Loving and her troupe Flash Parade, with Chic Kay, in their production of *Murder in the Red Barn*. I could not get a wink of sleep afterwards thinking about the bloody spade used to do the foul deed.

Oh yes, life was good. I had a loving family, plenty to do, grand holidays, and enough spectacle to spark anyone's imagination.

But when I turned twelve I had to go to secondary school at Synge Street. The Christian Brothers were a tough lot with a notorious reputation for brutality. Unlike Michael who followed me, I was not academic and was hopeless at sports. Days that had been filled with a sense of purpose and fun became bleak with beatings and fears of bullying. I endured five long years at that place before I took my Leaving Certificate exam and made my great escape.

Chapter 3

Look At Me, I'm Dancing

It is hardly an accident that I ended up with a career in show business. I've told you about my incredibly musical family. My goodness, when I think of it now, there was always someone practising scales and pieces on their instruments, entering Feis Ceoils, or mugging up on lines and learning songs for musicals or operas. The house hummed with eight burgeoning musicians. Now I would like to tell you about my mother's siblings.

Every Christmas the whole family loved to go to the pantomimes at the Gaiety or the Olympia where we would see the young Maureen Potter with Jimmy O'Dea, and we were brought to amateur pantos written and directed by my mother's brother, Pat O'Rourke, for the Bernadette Players in Rathmines. Pat's wife was the fine Irish actress Maureen O'Sullivan, not the Hollywood legend, but the Abbey player. She starred as Madge in the first production of Brian Friel's *Philadelphia, Here I Come!* at the Gaiety Theatre in September 1964. When the play premiered in New York in 1965, my aunt was persuaded to change her name to Mairín D. O'Sullivan to avoid any confusion with the Hollywood actress. She kept the name, and used it when she appeared as Auntie Rosie in the RTÉ television drama series *Glenroe* in the mid-1980s.

Maura and Joan O'Rourke, my mother's sisters, were members of the Longford Players in the Gate Theatre. From the time I was about seven, I was brought to see my two aunts in plays by Chekhov, Shaw, Wilde and Christine Longford. Joan was also the wardrobe mistress and we would be taken backstage after some of the plays where we might meet Iris Lawlor, Aiden Grennell, Anna Ferguson, Charles Mitchell or Dermot Tuohy. I loved the smell of greasepaint mingling with sweat, and the banter between actors as they slapped on cold cream to peel away the mask of their characters. Once, when I was at primary school at St. Mary's, we put on a production of *Who Killed Cock Robin?* and the pupils were very impressed when two 'professionals' (Maura and Joan) from the Gate Theatre came and did the makeup for us.

Aunt Joan got me my first real job in showbiz. It was 1958 and I was fourteen. Emmet Dalton Productions was filming *The Middle of Nowhere* with the great American actor and director John Cassavetes in Ardmore Studios. Joan rang my mother to ask if I could get off school for a week to be an extra, and she let me do it. I took the 86 bus to Bray each morning and walked the half-mile to the studios where filming began at 8.30 am. I was paid the magnificent sum of four pounds and ten shillings per day, extra for the one day we spent on location, and more again for the time I was asked to act as a stand-in. It was riches beyond compare and felt terribly glamorous.

After filming, I had to return to Synge Street. One of the 'Christian' brothers was zealous in his determination that I should not get the idea that I was anything special and beat me savagely with his leather strap. He made it his mission to make my school life as miserable as possible, and in that he was only too successful.

However, away from school I still had my hopes and plans. One of my ideas was to organise a day trip to the Isle of Man for the family. Some of Maura's friends heard about it and wanted to come too. Every Saturday I collected half a crown from each of them, and twelve weeks later I bought the sailing tickets. Dad dropped us to Sir John Rogerson's Quay where we met up with our friends. We were all excited. It was our first time on a ferry, the first time to leave the country. It went like a dream. We had a great time 'abroad' and returned home tired and happy.

In the late 1950s and early 1960s cinemas often had a short variety concert between the 'B' and 'A' films, and when I was sixteen Marie Tucker invited my sister Maura and me to take part in a show at the Apollo cinemas in Dundrum, Walkinstown and Sundrive Road. Married to the tenor Fergus Tucker, Marie was also his agent, and it was brilliant the way she could muster up concerts in which he featured. Our show included comedienne Catherine O'Connor and bass baritone Bill McMahon. There, too, was Ann O'Dwyer of Telefís Éireann's *Live at Three* fame (senior citizens were invited onto the programme and the floor managers used to call it 'Live at Three, Dead at Four'). Ita Flynn played the piano for us, and we had some really good costumes provided by Aunt Joan, who was then running the Rutland Wardrobe (the Longford Company were no longer working at the Gate). Each week we performed songs from different musicals. I did duets with Maura and Catherine and sometimes recited monologues. Although our show was slick and varied, it did not always go down well with the patrons who were impatient to see films like *The Apartment* or *Cleopatra* and not a sixteen-year-old rattling off a sentimental story. One night after our performance, they were especially rowdy and the manager said, 'It's like throwing cream buns to pigs!'

The monologues got a better reception when we performed for golf club functions, and on Sunday nights we would drive out to the Grand Hotel in Malahide to entertain British and American tourists. If Catherine was not available, my sister Ursula filled in for her, and the soprano Josephine Scanlon sang duets with Fergus Tucker from shows such as *Rose Marie* and *New Moon*. Marie was the MC for the shows. Marie had a broad Dublin accent that added a comical twist to all her links. One of her links went, 'Fergus and I 'ave 'ad air ups and dowins and when I do say to Fergus "Do it my way" Fergus done it his way,' at which point Fergus would burst into Frank Sinatra's 'My Way' which was a big hit at the time. At the end of the night we would come down from our stools on the stage where we had been perched all night and sing, '*Slán agus Beannacht*, Good night and God Bless You,' which disconcerted the British audience.

Whenever the girls or I were preparing for a competition or a performance, we always rehearsed with the wonderful Mrs Hayden who lived just around the corner from us. She taught me most of my music for exams at a cost of two shillings and sixpence an hour. Mrs Hayden was the organist at the Church of the Holy Name on Beechwood Avenue. For many years, Maura, Ursula, Patricia and I sang in the church choir and for weddings, and at Christmas we would always get a box of chocolates as a thank you from the priest. All my sisters were married in that church, and when Mam's sister Maura married a teacher, Paddy McNulty, in the same church, Patricia and I were trainbearers.

The bright lights were in my sights, I just didn't realise it. As an eighteen-year-old in 1962, freed from the torment of Synge Street, I took the first job that came along, that of junior clerk at the Liffey Hosiery Company in South William Street. A couple of months later I was offered a much better job in the accounts department of Brooks, Thomas & Co. Ltd., Builders Providers in Sackville Place where my facility with maths was put to good use. In those days it was unusual for a Catholic to work in Brooks, Thomas because most of the employees were Church of Ireland. To improve my prospects, I signed up for a night class at the Technical College in Rathmines, but then I received an offer I simply could not refuse.

Uncle Pat telephoned to say that he was looking for a pianist for a run of *The Rakes of Connemara* pantomime with the Bernadette Players, first in Rathmines and then on tour. Would I be interested? You can imagine the choice: sitting in an office all day poring over sawdust-dry figures and then heading off to classes for more of the same, or the smell of the greasepaint and the tinkle of the piano. So, instead of ingesting the finer points of accountancy, I attended rehearsals for the tour. My parents did not mind; after all, Pat O'Rourke was Mam's brother. I loved every minute of it and learned so much that was going to stand me in good stead in the future.

Aunt Maura's husband Paddy became principal of a school in Dundrum, and he was of a theatrical bent, too. When he put on children's musicals in the Marian Hall in Milltown, my sisters often performed and I played the piano, which was good experience too. Uncle Paddy also wrote plays *as Gaeilge* for Radio Éireann, but I was never in them.

It was around this time that I started taking singing lessons with Maura Tyrrell, a marvellous teacher who really stretched me, and when I was nineteen in 1963 I auditioned for Terry O'Connor, musical director of the Rathmines and Rathgar Musical Society. I wanted to be in the chorus of *The Student Prince*, and to say I was thrilled to be accepted is an understatement. The leading lady was the fabulous Louise Studley, who later became a dear friend. Ging's of Dame Street supplied our costumes. The week before we opened, the Curragh Musical Society had worn them in their production of the same musical. The costumes must have been used to remove makeup after their show because when they arrived to us they were filthy and the smell was dreadful. They were cleaned before we got into them, I can assure you.

On opening night, I was in the Gaiety Theatre as a member of the company in the feverish backstage atmosphere of bustling stagehands and pre-show nerves, selecting sticks of Leichner number 5 ivory for my face and number 9 rouge for my cheeks and applying crimson lake liner on my lips with a shaky hand. I was in my element. On stage, the greasepaint threatened to run under the intense heat of floodlights that had no filters, and the director kept reminding us to 'play to the footlights, play to the footlights'. At the time I thought it was the best production – ever!

Shortly after that, the Muckross Musical Society asked me to appear as Bunthorne in their production of Gilbert and Sullivan's *Patience*. I studied for the part with Mrs Hayden and enjoyed it hugely. So when the time came to enter for the Rathmines and Rathgar Cup at the Feis Ceoil in 1965, I sang

Bunthorne's aria 'Am I Alone and Unobserved', and I won! I was so excited that I rushed around to Mrs Hayden's house to show her my trophy.

Maura Tyrrell was training Patricia at the time, and the next year she entered Patricia and myself into the Feis Ceoil's Wilson Cup, awarded for the best excerpt from an opera. We performed a very difficult scene from *The Medium* by Gian Carlo Menotti. In this work, the singers are singing against the music all the time, so it requires a very good ear. We were both delighted to win, and when I failed to get anywhere in the oratorio competition I was not in the least upset – I already had prizes under my belt.

I was still living at home and helping out in the shop. Dad thought it would be a good idea if I could drive his van to make collections and deliveries. A cousin showed me the rudiments of driving and took me for a trial run in the country. It all seemed quite straightforward. On my return to the shop, Dad handed me the keys to drive home to Beechwood Avenue. I had not quite mastered pulling away, and when I took my foot off the clutch, the car jumped and cut out, but eventually I got going. The country run hadn't prepared me for stops and starts, and at traffic lights and intersections the car spluttered and jerked and I sensed the irritation of the drivers behind me. By the time I turned into Annesley Road in Ranelagh I was in a proper panic. I misjudged the width of my van and tipped off a delivery truck. The driver was very kind and said that because there was not much damage, he would let me go. Turning into Dunville Avenue I was still a bit shaky. Just beyond the railway bridge a lady had parked her car on my side and, instead of stopping to allow an oncoming car through, I decided to pass her. Meanwhile, the other car kept coming, so I had to pull in and I scraped the side of the lady's car. Catastrophe! I stopped and got out, stammered my apologies, and agreed to pay for repairs.

By the time I got home I was fit for nothing, but I had to turn around and drive back to the shop, terrified at having to confess everything to my father. Thankfully the shop was full of customers, so when I told Dad I'd had a bit of an accident he said he would take a look later. I grabbed my trusty bicycle and cycled home, uncertain of my fate. Luckily the van was strong and there was little damage, so, apart from the paintwork on the lady's car, I got off lightly. After that, I took lessons in an Austin Cambridge with the aptly named Mr Cambridge at the O'Connell Bridge Driving School. I bought an Austin Mini, and for years drove to shows all over the country. Nowadays, I take trains and buses. Let someone else do the driving.

During the 1960s I was asked to join the Muckross Musical Society. Muckross College was near where we lived so I could walk to rehearsals. This society gave me the opportunity to play leading roles in several musicals, including Ko-Ko in *The Mikado*, Jack Point in *The Yeomen of the Guard* and Timothy in Julian Slade's *Salad Days*. Eileen Knowles directed them all and she was also the chorus mistress for the R&R. Eileen was in her eighties when I started to work with her, but she was still a tough cookie. At rehearsals she would turn her back to the company and if anyone sang a wrong note she would swing around in her chair, point at the offender and shout, 'You sang an E flat!' For *Salad Days* I had to step up a gear or two, and learn to step it out. The story is a light-hearted one about a piano which, when it is played, makes everybody dance. Dolores Delahunty, the choreographer, made us all work hard to ensure that the dancing really enhanced the show. Ann Hodgins played Jane to my Timothy, and we got the award for best leads in a musical from the Association of Irish Musical Societies. I was invited back to the R&R for several shows, including *The New Moon, Bitter Sweet, Patience* and *The Mikado.* My final appearance with them was as the Duke of Plaza Toro in *The Gondoliers.*

I got my first chance of managing a musical at the suggestion of actor and singer Bill Golding, who was about to star in *Go Where Glory Waits Thee*, a new show about the life of Thomas Moore of *Irish Melodies* fame. I knew Bill slightly because the Goldings lived near our shop and I had played in pantos with his sister Mary. I leapt at the opportunity of learning more about the logistics of putting on a show and touring with it. I soon found out that managing meant reconnoitring venues (doing recces), planning the staging and lighting, arranging travel, accommodation and meals for the company and generally ensuring that everything ran smoothly. Maureen Charlton wrote the musical. It starred Bill with Louise Studley, and the accompanist was Louise's mother Eileen Studley, a wonderful pianist.

The show had a successful run in Avoca, County Wicklow but when we transferred to the Gorey Arts Theatre in County Wexford there was almost a calamity one night when a spotlight fell to the ground and fused all the lights in the theatre. Fortunately a nun in the front row had a torch with her. With great presence of mind she switched it on and beamed it up at Louise and Bill who, like the great troupers they were, kept on singing while Eileen played and I scuttled around backstage desperately trying to locate the fuse box. It seemed to take for ever to change the fuse and restore power, but I am assured it was about two minutes. Despite this hitch, Bill said I would make a grand show manager, which was a big boost to my confidence.

Years later, Eileen wrote a revue for the Gate Theatre which starred Milo O'Shea. One of her songs was 'Time on My Hands', which I still play at weddings. Maureen Charlton composed a musical based on Richard Brinsley Sheridan's *The School for Scandal* in which I played Benjamin Backbite in the Pavilion Theatre, Dun Laoghaire. When I was a producer of *Sunday Miscellany* on RTÉ Radio 1, Maureen wrote many scripts for me. Bill Golding gained a reputation for fine acting, and achieved nationwide recognition for the role of Rory on the children's television show *Wanderly Wagon.*

That stint of management was a foretaste of what was in store for me, but back in the sixties I was still stuck behind my desk in the accountancy office, and all the fun, hard work and pizzazz of the musicals belonged to another life, another me. I was a fairly diligent employee, but my head was filled with song. After six years working for Brooks, Thomas & Co. I did not see much prospect for change. But change was coming, and it was gonna be good.

Chapter 4

Schlittenfahrt on Radio

It was 1967. Uncle Paddy telephoned to say there was a job advertised in the *Independent* that might interest me. I dashed out, bought the newspaper and quickly scanned the Appointments page. RTÉ Radio was recruiting for a sound effects man to work in their drama department.

I almost danced on the street, but was immediately filled with self-doubt. Radio Éireann, as we always thought of it (although it had been renamed RTÉ Radio in 1966) was a living, breathing entity in the lives of every man, woman and child in the country. They relied on it for news, sport and entertainment. To be part of the organisation was an incredibly glamorous prospect and impossibly hard to attain. I knew I stood little chance, but I applied anyway, and was bowled over when I made it through the initial interview. I was taken on trial for six weeks to train in sound effects and as a disc jockey (the guy who changes the records for the presenter).

The radio station broadcast from offices high up in the General Post Office building on O'Connell Street. I was shaking with nerves on my first day. I walked through the great double doors on Henry Street, took the lift up to Reception, timidly announced who I was, and waited to be told what to do and where to go. I was directed to the Green Room beside Reception, which was the base for the actors and soundmen, and informed that a diary was essential to write down details of the duty schedules that were posted on the noticeboard two weeks in advance. The Green Room was on a long carpeted corridor that also had offices for heads of departments and engineers, a commercial office for the booking of advertisements, and a contracts department. Stairs led up to the GPO canteen, a facility that we were allowed to use. This seemed really handy, until the day I was on early duty and saw mice cavorting around the gas stoves. That put me off any ideas of eating lunch there and I limited myself to tea and toast in the morning, although I did not want to think too hard about the toaster.

There were eight of us on the course: two from Cork, one from Sligo and the rest of us from Dublin, but there were only four vacancies. One of our duties was to devise sound effects for the drama productions that were broadcast each week. I noticed that when recorded music was used during the play it often caused difficulties because it was hard to match it up with the dialogue. I offered instead to play the piano as an accompaniment. With the script in front of me, I could quicken the pace or slow it down to finish on cue with the performer. This was appreciated, and I earned a little extra money as well. After the six weeks I was interviewed again in both English and Irish for a permanent job. It quickly became apparent that my command of the Irish language was not great, so it was lucky that I had proved reasonably efficient, and that they realised my versatility on the piano was useful because it saved them from having to get a pianist. I was in!

With considerable relief I left my job in Brooks, Thomas – I doubt I was much of a loss to them.

The equipment in Henry Street was antiquated. If a tape machine or turntable stopped working, we had to telephone an engineer, who would arrive with a maintenance person to sort things out, hopefully in time for the next broadcast. When the lift broke down we had to climb about six flights of stairs. I did feel sorry for the more mature actors, but Aiden Grennell used to say it was good for the heart.

I was unbelievably excited to do my first broadcast as a disc jockey. I had to play the records for the presenters and run the advertisements on such programmes as *Rogha Na mBan*, *Hospital Requests*, *Pop Call* and *Morning Call*. The management at RTÉ were keen to promote the highest standards when it came to good taste and impeccable pronunciation. Úna Sheehy and Bridget Kilfeather listened to almost every word in the programmes to make sure they were all correct. If there was a foreign politician or a city with odd spelling, they would be consulted beforehand for the proper pronunciation, and no one dared to drop their 'th's! Despite their best efforts, however, many a gaffe, intentional and otherwise, was made on air. Having played a popular song, one lady announcer said, 'Well, there we leave Harry Belafonte with his hole in a bucket'. On another occasion a presenter was interviewing a man who had a met an actress famous for her lovely long legs and she asked him, 'Legs apart, how was she?'

Sometimes continuity announcers would daydream while a programme was being broadcast. On one *Sunday Game* there was a minute's silence in Croke Park for a well-known player who had died. The announcer suddenly realised that there was nothing on air, apologised for the break in transmission and hurriedly played a piece of céilí music. It was common then for fans to bring a transistor radio to Croke Park to listen to Micheál O'Hehir's commentary, so the minute's silence was destroyed as céilí music blasted all around the ground.

Maurice O'Doherty was a 'divil' and was always looking for ways to annoy the powers-that-be. He called me in to the continuity suite one day and said, 'Kev, wait 'til you hear this.' On air, he then proceeded to read, 'Our next piece of music is "Die Musikalische Schlittenfahrt" by Leopold Mozart.' Maurice of course put emphasis on 'Schlittenfahrt'. The head of speech standards was in like a shot, but there it was on the record sleeve and Maurice had a grin on his face like a Cheshire cat.

John Keogh was another of the 'Henry Street Villains'. In the era before air conditioning the studios would sometimes be very hot, so the announcers and presenter would often leave a window open. One day, just before the popular programme *Hospital Requests*, John brought some bread up from the canteen and spread crumbs on the windowsill. His audience was mystified by curious squabbling sounds, unaware that belligerent seagulls were scrapping for the crumbs.

John is an excellent musician with a great sense of timing. Listeners to the famous Kilfenora Céilí Band were accustomed to hearing the habitual two beats of the drumsticks before the band commenced each tune. John would allow the two beats, stall the record with his finger, tap the microphone with a ruler so that there were four beats and then let the record play.

As far as I can remember, no one ever caught on.

I worked for a while with Terry Wogan. Anyone who ever worked with Terry will tell you that he was exactly the same off air as he was on air. He was always up to tricks, like the day an announcer was ploughing her way through a long introduction to an orchestral concert, and to make her laugh he slowly began to unbutton the back of her blouse. Years later, when I was in London recording *This is Your Half-Hour Call*, I met him outside the BBC's Broadcasting House and we had a long chat, unwittingly attracting the attention of passersby. 'Would you look at those oul wans staring at us,' I said. 'I'll bet they're all saying who is that talking to Kevin Hough?' Terry just roared with laughter.

Shortly after joining the station, I decided to see if my singing voice could be developed. I was thrilled when Veronica Dunne agreed to take me on. I studied with Ronnie for three years. We found out fairly soon that my voice was not suited to opera, but she gave me invaluable lessons in technique, correct breathing and posture, and in how to hit the back of the auditorium on a noisy Wednesday matinée. Even more importantly, Ronnie became a very dear friend, and when we had both had enough of the scales, we would swan off for a chat and a gin and tonic.

In my early days with RTÉ the station closed down at 3.00 pm. This left me ample time to pursue my interest in music and theatre. I began to be offered roles by different musical societies such as Jack Point in *Yeoman of the Guard*, Njegus in *The Merry Widow*, Count Homonay in *The Gypsy Baron* and Green Carnation Boy in Noël Coward's *Bitter Sweet*.

In 1969 I received a telephone call out of the blue from Eily O'Grady. Eily was musical director of the Clann Gael Festival Singers, and they were due to embark on a three-month tour of Canada and the United States. The baritone soloist had pulled out at the last minute and she wondered if I would be interested in taking his place. Well of course I would, but I was thrown into a quandary for two good reasons. The first was that I didn't see how I would be allowed that much time off work. The second was that I had already bought my ticket to go to Kenya – yes Kenya! – in December. I, who had been no farther than the Isle of Man on a day trip, now had the possibility of travelling to two huge continents in the space of a few months. The two trips were an enticing but terrifying prospect. For days I went around in a state of nervous collapse, and when my boss, Tommy Warren, sent for me, I was prepared for a big disappointment. But he said that the personnel department had agreed to release me for the three months, and that I could still take my annual leave afterwards, provided there was no need to employ a replacement for the period. Eily's sister, Geraldine O'Grady, was leader of the RTÉ Symphony Orchestra at the time and I think 'strings' had been pulled. Tommy offered my duties to the staff on an overtime basis and they were delighted with the extra few bob.

Eily's husband Frank Patterson was the tenor on the tour; I was the MC and also had to sing a few songs. When we reached Tacoma in Washington state I lost my voice to some infection. I could go on stage and mime to the songs, and Frank agreed to read my MC's script, but it was not fair to the other performers, so after two days I suggested to the tour manager, Harry Rand, that I return to Ireland. He would not hear of it and instead arranged for me to see a doctor. That man was a miracle worker. Within a day I had my voice back, but I was warned not to take eggs, chocolate or milk, which are bad for the vocal chords. Several members of the company also took this advice, and we were all grand for the rest of the tour. So grand, in fact, that we often partied after the shows, which did not go down too well with the company manager, but we still gave one hundred per cent to our performances.

We were on stage in Hollywood one evening and I glanced across at Eily, who was playing the piano. She was a very pleasant person, but at that moment she had a face that would stop a clock, and there was murder after the show. The Irish dancers were wearing no knickers, and during a high-kicking hornpipe Eily had got an eyeful! Whether the audience were aware of this state of undress is not known, and the dancers were properly attired for the remainder of the tour. We travelled enormous distances. At the other side of the country we did a concert one night in Niagara. Next day the hard working dancers took a well-earned rest, although some did accompany us to visit the Falls.

Above the cascades roar and the click from the cameras of excited Japanese tourists, I heard one of them say to another, 'Jesus, me feet is killing me.'

'You're right,' said the other. 'Let's go back to the hotel. Sure, what is it, only water anyway!'

It was a time of great struggles for civil rights, both in Ireland and the United States. I have never been very politically minded but I have always had a strong sense of what is fair and right. I noticed that in the hotels or on the streets it was predominantly black people who did the menial work. Following our shows we would often be entertained to supper at the venue or in somebody's home. After one matinée performance, Harry Rand said that we had been invited to a grand house about three miles from the theatre, but that he was not going because he did not like the owners. Several huge cars came to collect us, and we had an enjoyable evening with superb food in a residence where most of the staff were black people. Later, the host gave harpist Eithne Dunne and myself a lift back to our hotel. I said to him how pleasant and courteous his staff had been. He said that the servants were fine but he did not like them in his house as they had their own peculiar smell. This statement so appalled us that Eithne tried to jump out of the moving car and I had to make a grab for her. Luckily, we were near the hotel, and when we left the car we did not even say goodnight or thank you – I think he got the message.

The tour was a terrific success, but no sooner had I touched down on Irish soil than I was off on my trip to Kenya. Father Bob Kelly had taught me at junior school and was a family friend. Before he went abroad on missionary work he had been a frequent visitor to our house for musical evenings and to play nomination whist with Mam, and he had issued a standing invitation for any of us to go and see him in Africa.

It was a freezing cold day in December when I got back from America. I just had time to go home, unpack my case and repack with light clothes and a Christmas pudding and other food goodies from Mam for Father Bob before heading out to the airport the next morning for a flight to Frankfurt. Frankfurt was blanketed in snow and I was glad of my cosy sheepskin coat. I caught the plane to Nairobi, and landed into glaringly hot and humid conditions. Suddenly my coat didn't seem such a good idea. Imagine my dismay when I was informed that my suitcase had gone missing. There was nothing for it but to swelter halfway across Kenya on a small

East African Airways plane to Mombasa, and trust that my case would follow on in a few days.

Bob met me at the airport and what could we do but laugh. I bought a shirt and shorts, and we drove about fifty miles along rough dusty roads to the Shimba Hills, and up a dirt track to the Holy Ghost Missions. Bob lived in a simple, four-bedroomed bungalow with two fellow Irish priests; other priests' houses were nearby. I hadn't slept for days what with all the travelling, and the sight of my own little room and a bed I could actually stretch out on was a blessed relief. When I awoke there were eggs and paw paw fruit for breakfast. Our cook lived in a typical village hut with mud walls and a roof of palm leaves, and he prepared very tasty meals for us with cold meats and cheese at lunchtime and a variety of home-grown vegetables at dinner. In the evenings we listened to records, mostly opera and light classical. The locals were always smiling, and they loved Bob because he played the mouth organ for them at impromptu music sessions.

After a couple of days we were informed that my suitcase had turned up. We returned to Mombasa, only to discover that the case had been invaded by ants who had eaten all the goodies and, worse still, the Christmas pudding! It was a terrible shame because it was the one thing Bob had been looking forward to.

The Shimba Hills region is a lush, tropical rainforest of rolling hills and coastal forests, with wild animals and, of course, mosquitos. Bob gave me a supply of malaria tablets and told me to be sure to arrange the mosquito net securely around my bed at night. Unfortunately, my bare arm was next to the net and the little feckers had a feast the first night. Despite my bites, I remembered to shake out my shoes in the morning in case poisonous spiders had taken up residence. The toilet was a large hole in the ground near the house. The priests used disinfectant sparingly since they did not want to kill off the creatures that ate the waste, and in that heat the smell from the privy would fell a stronger man than me.

Every day we went to different villages to visit the sick and say mass and offer whatever assistance we could. One day we had to go to a leper colony about twelve miles away. The very word 'leper' struck dread into my heart, but Bob assured me that the people we would meet had already been treated for the disease and were not infectious. When we reached the cluster of huts, several local nuns and nurses ran out to greet us with open arms – I expect they did not have many visitors. Bob said Mass for about 25 people and gave them his blessing. As we were leaving, I shook hands with some of the sufferers so as not to seem impolite, but the minute we were out of sight I rubbed my hands vigorously on my shorts, hoping I had not picked up the terrible affliction.

I awoke on Christmas Day 1969 to a piercing sun and a sky of intense blue. After breakfast we left the mission to travel five miles to a village where Bob said mass under a tree. He had invited two priests from another mission to our house for dinner, so that evening about eight of us sat down for our modest feast of chicken and vegetables from the garden and bottles of East African beer. We raised a toast to the absent pudding, and rounded off a very pleasant day by listening to recordings of all the Gilbert & Sullivan operettas (yes, I did say all).

I heard that a group of local people and a few priests from a nearby school were taking a trip to Tanzania to climb Mount Kilimanjaro, and Bob arranged that I get a lift in one of the jeeps. My first sight of the snowy peak was truly awe-inspiring, and daunting. It is the highest mountain in Africa, more than 19,000 feet above sea level. When we got there, I could not believe how many people, young and old, were heading up on the long, hard trek.

I was told it would take three days to hike to the summit and two days to come down (nowadays they take much longer). Porters carried our bags and at each stage we stayed in basic huts. The closer we got the summit, the colder it became, and I was not at all prepared for the weather conditions. I wore five pairs of socks and four underpants under my clothes and rain gear on top, and one guy kindly gave me a jumper. On the night of our last climb we left the huts at 11.00 pm, but I quickly realised that I would never make it all the way. I had been asthmatic as a child and I just could not get enough air into my lungs. I gave my camera to a priest to take photos for me at sunrise, and turned back to make my way down to the hut on my own. It was pitch black. I could hear strange animal noises, very like the cawing of magpies and the grunts of wild boar. I was terrified of being attacked and eaten by marauding lions. By the time I reached the shelter of the hut, my heart was pounding. I kept vigil for the rest of the group. They all made it safely up and down, and a couple of days later was I glad to have the luxury of a shower and a good dinner! I would never attempt anything like that again, but I am very proud of having climbed 16,000 feet up Mount Kilimanjaro.

A safer pursuit was snorkelling. The beach at Mombasa was gorgeous and the sea was crystal clear. I have never seen anything like the shapes, colours and sizes of the tropical fish. Afterwards, Bob went shopping and I took a walk along the white, sandy strand. Although it was not particularly sunny, it was very windy, and when we returned to the Shimba Hills I had blisters all over my arms from being burned. Another sleepless night.

One day we were called to a mother who was very ill after giving birth to her son. Mother and baby were at risk and Bob gave them a blessing. They both survived, and I was honoured and delighted when the mother named her boy Kevin, after me. That man would be in his forties by now. I would love to meet him and hope he has done well. Ever since my trip I have sponsored a child in Kenya; I have seen the difference even a little money and care can make.

Bob's brother Terry, who worked for British Airways in London, came to visit for a week and we had some great trips around the country with him. From the safety of our jeep we saw monkeys, hippos, rhinos and wonderful, stately giraffes, and once we had to stop to allow a herd of huge, oddly graceful elephants lumber across the road in front of us. One night we were invited to a house a field away from where we were staying, so we walked over. We were enjoying a cup of tea with our neighbour when a boy ran in to say that a lion had been seen nearby. A few more people gathered, Bob took out his mouth organ and I was asked to sing and the time flew by, but the dark walk back through that field seemed very long. Thankfully, the lion did not appear.

I never lost my fear of spiders and snakes. In one of the villages, Bob was saying mass when there was a lot of noise and excitement nearby. A cobra had slithered out from the undergrowth. Some of the local men caught it and swung it around and around before throwing it onto the road in front of a passing jeep.

At the end of my African adventure, I suggested that Bob should record some of the local music. He did gather material, and when he returned to Ireland a few years later, he and producer Cathal MacCabe prepared and broadcast a thirty-minute radio programme, *Heartbeat of Africa*.

It was an unforgettable trip. When I got home in January 1970, I had so many stories to tell. My colleagues welcomed me, and if they gave a backward glance to all the lovely over-time that ended once I resumed work, they were too kind to say so. As for me, after four months away in strange lands I was more than ready to take the dear old clunky lift up to Reception, and resume my life in the studios of RTÉ Radio.

Chapter 5

The Roar of the Greasepaint

I loved working on sound with the Radio Éireann Players. They were full of characters like Ginette Waddell, George Green, Conor Farrington, Daphne Carroll, Eamon Kelly, Pegg Monaghan, Brendan Cauldwell, Aiden Grennell and Florence Lynch. Florence was a very heavy smoker, and the tape recording had to be stopped over and over again so she could have a good cough. She owned a dog, and because she found it difficult to walk with her bad chest she used to exercise him by tying him to the back bumper of her old car and slowly driving through the Phoenix Park. I often wondered what would happen to the poor old dog if her foot ever slipped on the accelerator.

The *Sunday Night Play* inspired an interest in drama up and down the country, and the Players had won the coveted international Prix Italia award for best radio drama in 1961 and 1964. The actors rehearsed for four days; the fifth day was devoted to recording. When the play was live, the actors rehearsed all week and also on Sunday afternoon before the broadcast at 8.00 pm. I always thought the live shows were best because, just like theatre, the adrenalin kicks in and the performance has an edge, a freshness. The radio actor has the most demanding of all acting jobs. She/he has to get the character into the listener's living room with just voice and a microphone, and subtle sounds can change everything. A young actress was auditioning one day and she asked me how to play an old person. I advised her to breathe with difficulty. She had to read various ages through the audition and took my advice when it came to the elderly lady. She got the role.

I learnt so much about timing and intonation from those actors. It was fun devising sound effects, but I also had to be alert to extraneous sounds, such as traffic noise or seagulls or the old floorboards in Henry Street. If the play involved actors moving between microphones, we would have to soak towels in water and lay them on the floor to dampen the creaks. In one production, *Front Room*, the lead character throws all her kitchen delft against a wall. There was no sound substitute for that one, so I went to the GPO canteen, collected their chipped crockery and we had a smashing time in the studio, with some serious sweeping up afterwards. Deirdre O'Meara played the lead in that production and she was marvellous, but then, she had been involved with show-biz people all her life because her mother had a premises on St Stephen's Green called Madam Drago's Theatrical Wigs.

Auditions were held for RTÉ's 'Reach for the Stars' competition in 1971 and I decided to enter. If you glance at the photograph I sent in with my entry form you will think I was about seventeen, but I was twenty-seven! I sang 'Fanlight Fanny' and 'The Gentle Maiden'. Although they said very nice things about me – 'Excellent voice and presentation, good entertainer' – I was not what they were looking for and it went no further. But there was no time for disappointment. Eithne

Reaching for the stars with this audition photograph, 1971

O'Donnell, a good friend, asked if I would be interested in directing a play for the St Dominic's Past Pupils' Union Drama Society in Ballyfermot.

Directing? I was itching to give it a go! John O'Donnell's *Silver Wedding* was chosen to go on that June. The actors in the drama society were a grand group, and all of them local. I particularly remember Colette Cowlard and her great line: 'I will have a hot whiskey with plenty of ice.' What a comedienne – I hope she went into the profession. The convent hall had a fair-sized stage and very good stage management. They packed out the house for the run and we had an uproarious party on the last night. The following year I directed their production of *Shadow of a Gunman* by Seán O'Casey. Jack

Cruise's son Gerard designed the set for me. The players occasionally rehearsed at our house, and they all enjoyed my mother's tea and buns after the session. That play was a sell-out, too.

In the autumn of 1971 I was playing the small part of Rudi in Franz Lehár's *Land of Smiles* with the Glasnevin Musical Society at the Gaiety Theatre. At the same time, Jack Cruise was casting *Cinderella* for a run at the Olympia and could find no one to play Buttons. His friend Val Fitzpatrick saw me in the Gaiety and advised Jack to take a look. My show ended and, to expand my musical knowledge, I took an extra-mural course on Richard Wagner in UCD. I was halfway through the course when I received a call from Jack with an offer to play the part of Buttons. I happily abandoned Wagner and donned a bellhop hat.

Rudi in Land of Smiles, *1971*

Cinderella was an unprecedented success, playing to full houses for 13 incredible weeks. I would arrive for work in Henry Street at 6.30 am and finish at 1.00 pm, rush home, have a bit of sleep, grab some food and get off out to the Olympia for the evening performance. Wednesdays were tough. After work, I went straight to the theatre for the matinée and stayed on for the night's show before going home, exhausted, for a few hours' sleep before getting up at 5.30 am for work again. I loved it.

Buttons with Jack Cruise as the Ugly Sister in Cinderella, *1971*

However, during the run, events in Northern Ireland took a tragic turn. On Sunday, 30 January 1972, British troops opened fire on a civil rights march in Derry, killing thirteen people. The Irish nation was in shock. Most of the theatres in Dublin closed the following day, but Jack Cruise insisted we had to go on because we had a lot of bookings. Many of my friends from RTÉ were due to come, but cancelled – who could think of enjoyment at such a time? As Buttons, I had a lot of interaction with the audience, but what do you do when there is no audience? At one point I was supposed to throw buns and crisps at them, but I was throwing them into empty seats. We all felt awful, knowing we should not be on stage at all.

On another night a lovely little girl named Rachel Downes came to see the show for her seventh birthday. She fell in love with Buttons and was brought around to the stage door to meet me. I was thrilled to have an admirer. She asked where I lived and I told her and gave her my telephone number. Big mistake. She would phone when she got in from school just as I was having an afternoon nap between my shift and the evening performance, and I would have to talk to her as Buttons, not as Kevin! She asked me lots of questions and could not understand why Cinderella preferred the prince to me. She made so many calls that my mother suggested we invite her for afternoon tea. She arrived with the most stunningly beautiful blonde mother. My mother, well used to entertaining, put on a spread for them. I discovered that Rachel's father made the famous Downes Buttercrust Bread and that they lived on the Merrion Road. We talked for a good while. She was excited to be speaking to Buttons 'in the flesh', and I was amazed we got on so well together with an age gap of 20 years. Later she sent me her First Holy Communion picture and I still have it somewhere. Rachel, I hope you read this because you were my first and greatest fan.

I stayed with the Jack Cruise Company for three pantomimes and two variety shows. When I played the Genie in *Aladdin*, I had some really good numbers, one of which was with the Royalettes dance troupe. The famous Theatre Royal on Dublin's Hawkins Street had recently closed and Babs De Monte, Alice Dalgarno and the Royalettes had moved to the Olympia Theatre in Dame Street. Alice was a great choreographer and she gave me a fantastic routine in the show, despite the fact that I did not have the legs. Babs made me

The Genie flanked by a bevy of Royalettes in Aladdin, *1973*

a skin-tight costume, and to keep myself slim and fit I used to walk the three miles from home to the theatre each night.

I was telling my Aunt Joan about the costumes and about working with Babs and Alice, and she said they were known in the business as 'his and hers'. I had no idea what she meant, but she explained that they were a couple, so that was a bit of an eye-opener. After a few years in the business, I learned that there are a lot of his and hers out there, as well as his and his!

The dancers with the Royalettes were real characters. Rehearsals were well underway when my sister Fionnuala, who was a soloist with the company, found out that one of the girls was pregnant. The girl had not told Alice Dalgano about that; she knew Alice would not have taken her on for a long run because the costumes would have to be altered as the tummy got bigger. Fionnuala asked the girl if she was not worried to be dancing every night when she was expecting.

61

'Jaysus no,' came the reply. 'I have eight of them at home and danced on every one of them!'

One dancer used to lean on the girl next to her in the Can Can so that she could get higher kicks than anyone else. The other girls hated this and tried not to be beside her. During the dances the girls worked up a real sweat, and I often heard them in the wings afterwards saying, 'Hey Valerie, give's a loan of your BO spray'.

Alice Dalgarno once saw a Royalette in Dawson Street dressed in a fur coat and shaking a charity box. Alice was furious because she was not collecting for charity, but for herself! I spotted her at the Curragh Races up to the same trick and a lot of fellas were putting money into the box. That girl entered the 'Beautiful Eyes' competition at Butlin's Holiday Camp in Mosney and got through to the next round on the Monday night, a night when she should have been performing with us. She pleaded sickness and the other girls had to reorganise themselves so that the routine would work. She won the competition and her photograph was emblazoned across the *Evening Herald.* She was lucky to be let off with a very stern warning from Jack Cruise.

There is a scene in *Aladdin* where the two villains, Wishy and Washy, arrive to steal the jewels from the cave. I, as the Genie, had to jump off what was supposed to be a cliff. It was about 40 feet high, and as I took my leap I loved to hear the gasps of the audience, knowing that after I disappeared behind the set I would have a cushioned landing on a mattress. I was preparing to jump one night when I noticed that the stagehands had forgotten to position the mattress. What to do? I had to go for it, but some survival instinct made me grab the nearest rope on my descent, which happened to be holding up one of the flats. As I came down so too did half the set! The whole auditorium erupted into laughter thinking, no doubt, that I couldn't be much of a genie if I brought the house down each time I jumped.

'Tie a Little Knot in Your Pigtail' was one of my best songs in that show. I found it with help from Joan Smith of May's Music Store on Stephen's Green. All us Hough children had bought their exam music from Joan, and she was continually on the lookout for good comedy songs for me. When Joan moved from May's to the Gramophone Library in RTÉ, I and many other producers benefited from her amazing knowledge of music.

Costumes for the shows were hired from Burke's of Dame Street, next to the Olympia. Burke's was like an Aladdin's cave itself, with everything from top hats to glass slippers and everything in between – makeup and gowns and breeches and tiaras. The Bourkes were a large and famous theatrical family whose costumier business dressed all the major theatres and amateur dramatic societies in Dublin and many in the provinces too. I liked dealing with Katherine Burke, or Kotchie, as she was known; she was a great personality and a very resourceful lady. The story goes that in 1943 when Laurence Olivier was in Ireland to film scenes from Shakespeare's *Henry V*, he needed chain mail for the battle sequence. In wartime Dublin metal was in short supply, so Kotchie sent her young brother around the city to scrounge for any heavy twine he could find. She had the twine loosely knitted into garments and then painted them silver to create the desired effect. Her reputation was made! Many is the time I called on Kotchie to help me out with one costume, or 50 costumes, and she never let me down.

In *Jack and the Beanstalk* I played Carl, the second Principal Boy. The show was on over Christmas and into February 1974. The lovely Patty Ryan was the Principal Boy, Jack. At the end of the first act Jack had to climb the beanstalk into the land of the giant. There was only one snag: Patty was scared of heights. The beanstalk was made of very heavy coiled springs and, during rehearsals, Jack Cruise, a big man, tried to reassure her by climbing it; nonetheless, she remained terrified. As all the cast were gathered around singing 'Beyond the Blue Horizon', Patty had to start her climb. I was next to her on stage, and for every performance of the run she would turn to me, roll her eyes to heaven and mutter, 'I hate this fucking beanstalk!'

Holiday Hayride was a summer variety show in the Olympia, and we took it to the Cork Opera House and the Savoy Theatre in Limerick. One of the acts originated in the French circus: Janek and Dolena balanced and spun plates on tall canes. The plates had a hole in the middle and were specially made in France. The trick was that they started with one and ended up with about 24 plates spinning as they ran around the stage to music. Janek did most of the work while Dolena fed him the plates and pointed out the ones that were about to fall. The audiences loved it, especially when a plate crashed to the ground.

Every time a plate was broken Dolena would charge up to Jack Cruise's dressing room afterwards screaming, 'Mr Cruise, Mr Cruise, the music is too fast. We are *artistes*, not mechanics.' Jack would send for the musical director, Chris, and Dolena would repeat that they were *artistes*. Chris, cool as ever, would insist that the music was the same as the previous night. 'These plates are special!' Dolena would scream even louder. 'They come from France and if this keeps up, we will have to import more and this will cost much money.' The plate act allowed the rest of us to make a costume change in our dressing rooms in readiness for the next number. By the time we got to Cork, the plates were reduced to eleven, and we were reduced to a quick change in the wings.

A juggler from England was engaged for a guest spot at the Olympia. Her boat was delayed and she arrived just in time to give her music to the musical director and go on stage. She certainly looked the part in her sparkly costume, and as she valiantly threw silver hoops into the air we had high hopes. She could hardly catch one of them. The stage is raked, so each missed hoop rolled down into the orchestra pit among the members of the band. Next, she brought out tennis rackets and members of the band had to take evasive action to avoid being walloped on the head. But when she produced the tennis balls, they came flying across the stage and the whole band ducked. The audience found it uproariously funny – I am sure they thought it was all part of the act – but she was on the next boat back to England and never heard of again.

When each season finished at the Olympia, a few of us from the Jack Cruise Company were invited to perform at the Green Isle Hotel on the Naas Road, twelve miles from the centre of Dublin. Some people called it the Green Vile but I absolutely loved it. The manager, Tony Rooney, booked us for a seven-night gig starting on Sunday and finishing the following Saturday night. A few months would pass and we would get the call again.

There were two function rooms: the Ivory Room, where we played every night, and the ballroom, in which a dinner dance was held on a Saturday. So, on the Saturday my first gig was in the Ivory Room and then I would hurry to the ballroom to start the show there and await the arrival of the big-name star they brought on as an added attraction. I was always on the bill with a well-known singer, who later made a name for herself on television. I had a tried and tested medley of favourites, opening with 'One of Those Songs', and going on to 'Blue Heaven', 'Makin' Whoopee', 'Blue Skies' and 'Alexander's Ragtime Band'. As I was in the ballroom, my co-star would be in the Ivory Room, and then would join me for a rousing completion to the entertainment. We had not played together for a while and one Saturday night she asked if she could reverse the order and do the ballroom first. I of course agreed. After I had finished in the Ivory Room, I was standing outside the ballroom waiting for my cue to join her when I realised, to my horror, that she was singing my medley, song for song. Luckily, I had brought lots of music with me and had plenty of tunes in my head so was able to change my programme, but I thought it was the meanest thing to do to a fellow professional.

Fortunately, such incidents are rare, and many of the people I work with have become the greatest of friends. I met Catherine Walshe when she was the Fairy Queen in *Cinderella*. During the summer she would sing and play the fiddle at the banquets in Dunguaire Castle near Kinvara in County Galway. She and another soloist, Ann Meagher, shared a house down there. I often stayed and enjoyed their parties and travelling around Clare and Galway with them. On one occasion they were asked to entertain the press and some local dignitaries at the Oyster festival in Clarinbridge. The 'stage' was a few planks resting on some beer kegs. During the performance the whole thing collapsed and all the audience could see were legs flying up in the air. No one was hurt and we laughed all the way back to Kinvara.

I caught some of Catherine's shows at Dunguaire, but she told me about a memorable one that I missed. The performers had to wait on table as well as do the show, which could be a tough job, especially with difficult American customers, and they were not beyond spilling soup on a truculent guest and then apologising profusely. But one night Catherine overheard an American lady shouting at her husband Henry to take his pills. Well, Henry obviously did not because the next thing was that he toppled over and died. The show was brought to an abrupt halt and, as his corpse was carried onto the stage, the wife commented, 'Gee, it's gonna cost me a fortune to get him home'.

When I was not on stage in the Olympia, I was in the audience. To watch good performers doing their job well is an education. One show I especially remember was *Salad Days*, presented by a small touring company, each of whom had two or three roles, and all joined in the ensemble performances. It showed me what could be achieved with talented and versatile players. I learnt from bad productions, too. *Grab Me a Gondola* and *Dearest Dracula* spring to mind, although that had one number called 'Come into my Crypt' sung by female vampires in the flimsiest of dresses which saved the whole production.

Dick Condon was the manager of the Olympia Theatre during my time there. He was a thorough gentleman and a real professional. He not only worked hard in the theatre, but once a week he gave a rundown on theatrical events around the country on Gay Byrne's programme *Music on the Move*.

One evening, while we were doing *Cinderella*, Dick came to my dressing room and said, 'Kev, those black hairpins against your white bellhop's hat don't look well. Get some white ones.' It was a lesson for me because that is the kind of minor but important detail that the director should have spotted. Dick left the Olympia to manage a theatre in Norwich. He ran supper/theatre nights there and brought in huge audiences. My sister Fionnuala was singing with English National Opera North at the time. They played Dick's theatre in Norwich and she remarked to me that it was particularly well run. I have often thought that his talents were neither well regarded nor put to good use in Dublin.

During the three years I was with Jack Cruise we travelled to festivals and performed at functions as well as doing the five major shows. All that time I was holding down my job in Henry Street, but only with the great understanding and cooperation of my boss Tommy Warren. He arranged my duties in such a way that I could appear in those productions. I never missed a theatrical performance or my shift on the radio.

Chapter 6

Play Me a Song

After five years in the sound effects department I was offered the position of sound engineer. This was an opportunity to advance in my career, but it would involve doing live and recorded programmes that had to be manned at night as well as during the day. It was going to be impossible to combine that job with working on the stage. I went to Jack Cruise and asked his advice. He said I should leave his company and concentrate on RTÉ, because if I turned down the new job I would never be promoted again. It was, may I say, sound advice.

Shortly after my promotion in 1974, RTÉ Radio moved out of Henry Street to swanky new purpose-built buildings in Montrose, Donnybrook. The studios were fantastic and the equipment was top of the range. Stereophonic sound and FM radio was being introduced, and we went on a training course that was run by an engineer from the BBC.

Continuity announcers were the last to leave Henry Street and they were itching to get to the new studios. Treasa Davison was fed up waiting for the move, so she decided to break one of her announcements with a sharp intake of breath and a deep sigh followed by a long pause, before exclaiming that a mouse had run across her desk! Next day, of course, it was all over the newspapers. There was a rapid departure to Montrose after that.

My office was in one of the open plan sections in the centre of the building, and, although I was next to a window, none of those windows opened. The managers and heads of staff had offices around the sides of the structure. The studios were all underground so there was no daylight, and the air-conditioning was not great, which was a problem for some people. Occasionally, the RTÉ Concert Orchestra walked out because it was just too cold for them to play.

As sound engineer I had to balance the sound on live shows, set up microphones for guests, bring in outside broadcast reports and carry out the producer's instructions. I also had to edit recorded programmes. The new equipment and systems were highly technical, whereas I wasn't, so it was tough going at first, but I stuck at it. Someone must have been looking out for me, because my first assignment with sole responsibility was with Ciarán Mac Mathúna on his Sunday morning radio series *Mo Cheol Thú*. Ciarán never raised his voice, so there were no problems with balancing, and he was incredibly patient. If anything went awry, we just stopped the recording and started again.

As soon as I got the hang of my new job I really began to enjoy it, while still taking on any gig that would fit in with my schedule at RTÉ. I had played and sung at parties and weddings for my family and friends, and for soirées with Aunt Joan and her theatrical friends like Cyril Cusack and Micheál Mac Liammóir, and was always open to offers.

One day I received a phone call from a young woman called Maria Belotti, who asked if I would sing at her wedding in Phibsborough Church. She requested 'Ave Maria', 'Panis Angelicus', 'Nearer My God to Thee' and 'There's a Place for Us' from *West Side Story*. The organist was to be a Miss Harold and I was to telephone her to arrange for a rehearsal. About two weeks before the wedding I called the number. A sharp voice answered 'Housing', and I realised I was on to the Dublin Corporation Housing Department. I asked for Miss Harold. 'Speaking'. I explained that I was the singer for the wedding and she enquired what numbers I was going to do. I said 'Ave Maria', to which she replied 'Gounod or Schubert?' She thought 'Nearer My God to Thee' was more appropriate for a funeral, and then she said she had never heard of 'There's a Place for Us'. She said we did not need a rehearsal – we would meet up half an hour before the wedding.

Brian Mulvihill from RTÉ was going to record the wedding. He and I were there early but Miss Harold arrived with only 20 minutes to spare. I had borrowed the music for the *West Side Story* song from my sister. When Miss Harold saw it, a look of horror crossed her face, but at that stage the guests were filtering into the church.

The bride was a charming young woman, it was her big day, and I began to be really worried that the music would not be up to scratch. The battle commenced between organist, instrument and singer, and battle it was. The 'Panis' and the 'Ave' were okay but when it came to 'There's a Place for Us', you could forget it. It must have been the first time Miss Harold had grappled with it and we were never together. She was playing in Burgh Quay while I was singing in the key of E Flat. I could see the guests turning around and looking up. Of course, no one ever blames the organist, just the poor singer. While the bride and groom were signing the register, the good lady took off her organ-playing slippers, put on her street shoes and marched down into the church, tapped the best man on the shoulder, and demanded the fee for the musicians. She then paraded along the aisle waving an envelope up at me and shouting, 'I have your money for you, I have your money for you'. Hot with embarrassment I tried to hide behind one of the pillars. I heard later that she had been playing the final organ piece at a previous wedding when the bridal party had driven off without paying her, and she was not going to let that happen again. I cringed when I heard Brian's recording and promised myself I would never do another wedding, but of course I did. Surely it could never be as bad as that again?

A prominent judge asked me to play at his daughter's wedding. He said he had a good German upright and that he would have it tuned in readiness. The reception was to be in a marquee in the garden of the family home. Every piano is different and I like to get a feel for each one, so on the day of the wedding, and a wet, miserable day it was, I arrived early to check on the piano. When I entered the marquee, the first thing I saw was the piano getting drenched from rain pouring in through a hole in the ceiling. I quickly got five waiters to move it to a dry location, and then I took a closer look. It was little more than the kind of battered instrument you would find in the corner of a village hall. The ivories were all chipped and it was as tuned as a drunken singer leaving the pub at midnight. This gig was going to be very hard work.

The guests arrived and I did my best to play them in joyfully as they took their seats. During the meal I performed my set, which included a fast piece that ended with a fancy *glissando.* I swept my thumb up the notes, and suddenly there was blood everywhere – my thumb was in shreds from the jagged keys. A kind waiter fetched bandages for me and I was patched up sufficiently to continue for the agreed three hours before I could thankfully close the lid. I was then made to wait for my fee. In front of a number of guests at the bar, the father of the bride dug his hands into his pocket and produced a wad of notes. After asking what he owed me, he peeled off a few. Out of the place I thought I would never get, so I ran for the car and fled.

At a wedding reception in the Grand Hotel in Malahide, I was supposed to accompany several accomplished singers. When they turned out to be nervous novices, my heart sank, but we ploughed on valiantly. Then an old aunt was asked to get up and sing her party piece. 'Ah no,' she said, longing to be persuaded. After a little coaxing, up she got and sang 'Vilia' from the *The Merry Widow.* The guests clapped and cheered, and after that there was no stopping her. 'What'll we do next?' she asked me, and she was off on a Percy French medley. At the end of her fourth song, she turned and mentioned the name of another. I pretended not to know that one, and at last she sat down. Yet again, I swore to myself that I would never play for another wedding. Will I ever learn?

I have sometimes received unusual invitations. Not so long ago I was asked to entertain customers in Clerys Department Store on Dublin's O'Connell Street. In the 1940s, '50s and '60s it was quite normal to have live music in the shops. Peggy Dell played piano in Cavendish's furniture shop on Grafton Street; there was a trio in Robert Roberts' Café and a piano player in the Ship's Grill. Bay Jellett had a trio that played chamber music at the Dublin Horse Show. If it was a windy day, they held the music on the stands with clothes pegs, and if it was a cold day the ladies wore slacks under their long black dresses. The Gate Theatre also had a pianist, but the darling of them all was Tommy Dando and his Lowry organ in the Theatre Royal. When I was a child, I just loved to watch the big screen and sing along with the little dot bouncing along on top of the words to make sure the audience kept time.

It was such a grand old tradition that when Clerys' invited me to play the piano during one of their sales, I was delighted. I started at two o'clock and was joined by Mrs Guiney, wife of the owner. Somehow or other, the dealers in Moore Street got wind of the event and soon there was a crowd gathered around the piano. As more customers gravitated towards the music, Tom Rae, the company secretary, sensibly told me to take a coffee break. One of the dealers poked me in the ribs and asked, 'Hey son, when will you be back?'

When I returned, I bumped into a neighbour from Churchtown who asked me to play 'Can't Help Lovin' that Man of Mine' while she sang, and I obliged. Then I got a wallop that nearly knocked me off the stool from another lady who demanded 'Molly Malone' which she belted out with gusto and, with that, the thing turned into a proper knees-up. It cannot have contributed much to Clerys sales, however, because I was not invited back.

I never pass up an opportunity to see my friends perform if I can help it. In 1979, during one of the hottest summers ever, John Conroy told me he was doing a summer season in Newquay Theatre, Cornwall, so as soon as I had a few free days free I flew over. John's sister Wendy and cousin Amanda were there for a short holiday and I booked into the guesthouse where they were staying, run by the deliciously named Dorothy Duprée.

Dorothy had a sideline selling ices and sweets at the Cosy Nook, a small theatre on the seafront. Top of the bill for their show was a comic who was also lodging with Dorothy, so on John's night off, we all went along to the Cosy Nook to support him. We purchased our tickets from a woman who looked like a character out of a play herself with eccentric clothing and heavily waxed eyebrows, and when we were told she wheeled her two-legged dog around the town in a super-market trolley, we could well believe it.

It was a very poor house, and we were soon to discover why. It opened with a recording of Frank Sinatra's 'Nancy with the Laughing Face', during which the pianist walked down through the audience and proceeded up steps to the stage. She stumbled on her long skirt but recovered herself sufficiently to make it to her piano. Knowing that the audience would be familiar with the Ealing comedy star Peggy Mount, she announced that she was Nancy Mount, Peggy's older sister. Nancy started off the show with 'I Love a Piano' from Irving Berlin's *Easter Parade*. When she got to the part in the song where she had to spell out P-I-A-N-O she sang P-A-I-N-O. John nudged me and we tried not to giggle. There was worse to come. She said she was going to play 'The Sting' from the movie *The Entertainer*, which should have been the other way around, and to finish she declared that we were off to Russia with 'Hava Nagila', which of course is an Israeli folk song. It was hit and miss on the ivories too, and sadly she scored on the miss side of things. After Nancy, there were gypsy violins and jugglers, and a fire-eating act that nearly caused a conflagration.

What with the flames on stage and the hot night and no air-conditioning, the theatre was stifling, and it was a relief when the interval lights came up. We bought ices from Dorothy and wondered what the second half would bring. An elderly music hall soprano Roberta Pett (the wife of the producer Jerry Jerome) came on stage to sing 'It's My Mother's Birthday Today'. At one point during the number she left the stage with a bunch of flowers and headed for a lady in the audience. I think the lady in question had a few drinks on board, and when the singer handed her the flowers, the old girl hollered, 'I'm not your mother!' Undeterred, Roberta returned to the stage to sing the Judy Garland song 'I Was Born in a Trunk'. When we heard someone comment that maybe she should have stayed in the trunk we got a fit of the giggles and were worried that Dorothy might see us. The comic from her guesthouse finished off the evening, in more ways than one. He clearly loved himself, but he was an average performer with stock English jokes that we found unfunny. It must have been one of the worst shows I've ever seen, but whenever I meet Wendy and Amanda we have a good laugh about that night, so it was worth the price of the ticket.

The show at Newquay Theatre was in a different league with a billing of first-class performers. John is a terrific dancer and puts over his material so well. He sang numbers from musicals and a Percy French selection with great style and lots of movement. I had a lovely break from the radio and my own battle with the ivories, and even got a suntan.

Chapter 7

To Whom It Concerns

Every Saturday night along the highways and down the byways of Ireland, people switched on their television sets to watch the owl take flight, hear the immortal words 'Ladies and gentlemen, to whom it concerns', and settle back to be amazed, amused, shocked and entertained by *The Late Late Show* on Telefís Éireann. For almost 40 years from the early 1960s Gay Byrne, the show's suave presenter, tackled the thorny subjects of sex, religion and politics with such an engaged and professional manner that he helped to pave the way for some of the greatest cultural and social shifts the country has ever faced. There was entertainment as well, with musicians and well-known people with stories to tell. Throughout all that time Gay had regular programmes on radio, many of which I worked on, and I am happy to say that I shared the stage with him several times. For my first appearance on television, the worlds of radio and television coalesced for an evening of reminiscence and festivity.

In 1975 RTÉ Radio celebrated 50 years of broadcasting to the nation, and to mark the auspicious event the *Late Late* presented a special show on 15 November. All kinds of personalities who had worked in radio over the years were featured: Bernadette Plunkett, one of the first presenters; Din Joe and Rory O'Connor, who succeeded in the seemingly impossible – bringing Irish dancing to the radio with *Take the Floor*; actors from the Radio Éireann Players, including Ronnie Walsh, Joe Lynch and Brendan Cauldwell, who later performed a short scene from a comedy. Paddy Crosbie recalled 'funny incidents' told by children on *The School Around the Corner*. Albert Healy and Molly Phillips performed a piano duet, and the wonderful Joe Linnane played us out on the piano with 'Easter Parade'.

Gay wanted viewers to get an idea of what happened inside their wireless sets, or rather, back at the radio studio. Although I had left the sound effects department, I was happy to demonstrate this feature of dramatic productions. A microphone and some 'highly technical' tools of the trade had been set up behind a screen. I nipped in behind it and rubbed large wads of cotton wool together (walking through snow), then gently gyrated two sticks in a basin of water (rowing a boat, or lake water lapping), scrunched a rickety wastepaper basket (creaking bed) and shuffled old celluloid tapes from hand to hand (crackling fire, or strolling through a leafy wood). For the most part everyone was baffled, so I explained that it all made perfect sense when heard in conjunction with the action and dialogue of a play. It was great fun, and the next day people stopped me on the street to say, 'I saw you on the *Late Late* last night'. Fame at last!

I was working on such diverse radio programmes as *The Gay Byrne Show*, *Terry Awhile* with Terry Wogan, *Sunday Miscellany*, *Between Ourselves*, *Morning Call* and others when RTÉ announced they were going to launch a pop music station in 1979, and were recruiting for fresh, talented producers. I seized the opportunity and applied. You know what they say about buses? By coincidence I was offered a major promotion to the position of senior sound engineer in Radio 1 at the very same time. The job entailed working with the drama department, and on outside broadcasts and with the RTÉ concert and symphony orchestras, and it came with a huge hike in salary. But I was exhilarated by the prospect of new challenges, and when I went into Tommy Warren's office, he held out two envelopes with the job offers, knowing which one I would take. He was very good about it, saying that, although I was a big loss to his team, he wished me nothing but the best.

So, it was another six-week training course for me, and this one for the role of radio producer, in which I knew I could put all my enthusiasm and initiative to good use. To catch the attention of younger listeners the punchy slogan for the new station was: 'Radio 2 Comin' atcha'. Soon I was working on lots of programmes and running from pillar to post like a headless chicken, but I was a happy chicken. One of my first tasks was to find new voices for *Ireland's Choice*, a programme that featured music requests from listeners to our provincial studios. I travelled to Galway, Sligo, Cork, Waterford, Belfast and Limerick to audition guest presenters. Val Joyce was the anchorman in Dublin, and each presenter got fifteen minutes in the three-hour programme to broadcast the requests they had gathered. We alternated the studios every second week. It proved to be tricky on occasion because we never knew when a line might go down or a technical glitch occur, but it was a great idea. People just loved hearing their names on radio and the listenership numbers soared. I was also producing Brendan Balfe's *Golden Oldies* show on Sunday afternoons, and we kept the local record companies happy with Arthur Murphy's *The Best of the Irish* show that promoted Irish artists. Both Brendan and Arthur were seasoned professionals, but some of the newer presenters were inexperienced, and I asked Úna Sheehy and Bridget Kilfeather to coach them on using their voices and developing their broadcasting skills.

One person who needed no such coaching was Ruth Buchanan, who had been a continuity announcer before becoming a presenter. By great good fortune I had got the plum job of producing the flagship children's show on the new station and Ruth was chosen to present it. *Poparama* was fun from start to finish. Ruth was the ideal person for it, energetic and upbeat, and she was a marvellous help to me.

Ruth and Kevin, in a mad dash for Poparama

Many people who are now household names cut their broadcasting teeth co-presenting *Poparama* with Ruth, including Ian Dempsey, Simon Young, Jimmy Greeley, Geoff Harris and Barry Lang. Billy Brown, who had been a leading member of The Freshmen band, wrote the signature tune for the programme. Billy was into wildlife in a big way and was keen that children should appreciate the natural world. Every Sunday he came into studio to give a talk called 'Wildwatch'. He is also a fantastic artist, and when he gave me one of his paintings, I felt so lucky to have such a friend. I can claim to have given a certain Ryan Tubridy his first break as a book reviewer when he was just twelve. Trish Taylor Thompson, who now broadcasts on Lyric FM, also started out as one of our book reviewers.

The producer's lot is considerably lightened when he or she has an efficient broadcasting assistant, and I have had some of the best. My first BA in Radio 2 was Noreen Nichol from Kilkenny, and what a worker she was. The BA is responsible for a good deal of administration, such as ensuring that contracts for all the contributors to a programme are signed and that payments are made afterwards. The BA meets guests and puts them at their ease by offering tea or coffee before bringing them to the studio. We ran a matchstick model competition in association with Maguire & Patterson and Noreen was inundated with entries. All you could see in the Radio Centre were flimsy constructions in every shape and form – ships, castles, lighthouses, birds – that everyone had to oh so carefully walk between when getting to and from their offices. The graphic artist Billy Bolger was our judge and how he assessed them all I do not know. When the lad with the most marvellous model won, I tried to get him on

The Late Late Show. That did not pan out, so I arranged for his photograph to appear in the *RTÉ Guide.* The models were due to be collected by a certain date, the remainder were sent to charity, and it was a great relief to see the Radio Centre cleared and back to normal again. Some models were sent to Our Lady's Hospital for Sick Children, and I often sent tapes of our programme there as well because the children enjoyed them so much. Noreen Nichol left me to marry a baker from Waterford, and all these years later we still talk every week on the phone.

Over the years I have had many assistants, and they were so important in my life and in my work and I would like to name them all: Noreen Nichol, Pauline O'Donnell, Joan Torsney, Helen Howard, Catherine Maher, Deirdre Ryan, Deirdre Magee, Lucia Proctor, Sinéad Renshaw, Moya Doherty, Linda Bent, Jane Reid, Geralyn Aspill, Fionnuala Hayes and Deirdre O'Grady. I see or hear from most of them from time to time, and each has a special place in my memory.

One of my BAs had a curious filing system. I got a call from the mother of a prize winner complaining that after four weeks her child's prize had not yet arrived, although they had been waiting for it in the post every day. I apologised and promised to look into it immediately. I asked my assistant about it. 'Oh yes,' she said. 'It's in my pending file. I'll get around to it later.' I begged her to sort out the file, as the stack seemed to be getting larger every day. Apart from that she was a great help, and went on to become a writer of comedy material.

Phone-ins from the public were a popular part of radio programmes, and a BA is often the person they talk to first. I was passing near the *Gay Byrne Show* office one day when the phone was ringing. There was no one around to answer it so I lifted the receiver. 'It's a disgrace,' shouted a woman caller. 'I'm sick of Gay Byrne giving away coloured televisions to unmarried mothers in Coolock!'

We gave out some marvellous prizes on the show, even better than a television. An unforgettable prize came about through my great friend Anne O'Callaghan, who looked after public relations for Ryanair. She offered to fly a whole plane full of children to Mora in Sweden so that they could go to Tomteland, the snowy wonderland resort with Santa Claus, reindeers, games, stalls and cartoon characters, all geared for one-day visits. As you can imagine, we had thousands of entries for that, and on a Sunday morning in December the lucky winners assembled in Dublin airport for take-off. A young child came all the way from Cork, but when we

Anne O'Callaghan, flying high!

were called to the departure gate, she panicked and ran back crying to her mammy. The parents were devastated because there had been big excitement at home and they had driven such a long way.

On board the plane, Ian Dempsey and the puppet duo Zig and Zag provided non-stop entertainment. We had one minder for every four children, so that when we reached the resort everything went smoothly. After a slap-up meal in a log cabin, the children played games, explored the forests, saw elves and trolls and took a sleigh ride. They visited the Christmas workshop and left important messages with Santa. As the moon was rising in mid-afternoon I played carols on the piano and we rounded off the trip with a sing-along. There were lots of sleepy heads on the return flight to Dublin, and not all of them were children. We arrived back at 9.30 p.m, and it was only after all the children had been safely collected that we adults could relax and reflect on an extraordinary day. Back in studio the next morning, I thought of the little girl who had got no farther than the airport. I sent her a goody bag with a note to say how sorry we were and that we missed her.

Jean Darling, known as Aunty Poppy, was a real favourite on *Poparama*. Each week she kept our young listeners en-thralled with her stories. She also read them to children at venues all over the country and in Dublin Zoo, always dressed up in a period costume and a flowery bonnet. She looked charming and was so sweet with the girls and boys. Jean was an American actress who had been a child star in 1926 at the age of four. She appeared in dozens of silent films, including the *Our Gang* series, and in 1945 she played the role of Carrie Pipperidge in the premiere of *Carousel* on Broadway, which

ran for more than 850 performances. During rehearsals for
that show, she knitted a scarf
for the composer Richard
Rogers. Jean moved to Dublin
in the mid-1970s and worked
as a journalist and writer, and
then on to our programme. I
am proud to say that I share
something in common with
Richard Rogers: Jean knitted a
scarf for me, too, and it is one
of my treasured possessions.

Aunty Poppy (Jean Darling)
(Photo by John Cooney, RTÉ Archives)

In 1981 I got an idea for
a national children's song-
writing competition. It
proved to be one of the most
demanding and long-running projects we ever embarked
upon with *Poparama*. That autumn, I travelled around the
country searching for talent and encouraging anyone under
the age of eighteen to enter. When we began, Earl Gill was
my musical director, and one of the great draws of the contest was the fact that the children would get to hear their
songs performed by top-class professionals such as Tony
Kenny, Eileen Reid, Kathy Nugent, Rita Connolly, Brendan
Grace, Tina, Sandy Jones and Paul Duffy. The finals of the
first show were broadcast live on radio in February 1982.
When Billy Brown became musical director, we increased
the age limit to twenty, which had the desired effect of raising
standards, and when Chris Kenevey took over from Billy he
suggested that the contestants should sing their own songs.

That worked like a dream, and it was wonderful seeing those gifted young people giving it their all. Those who could write songs but not sing them were allowed to nominate a friend to perform for them.

After its first few years, the contest left the umbrella of *Poparama* but continued on 2FM, thanks to the generous sponsorship of Yoplait Ireland and then Jacobs Biscuits. Jane Reid was my broadcasting assistant then, and became heavily involved in making arrangements and designing programmes for the competition, and in keeping our sponsors happy with their profile in the contest.

The tenth anniversary was a significant milestone, and in the autumn of 1991 we held a party to launch the 2FM/Yoplait Song Contest at Shannon's Restaurant, Stillorgan. It was a glitzy occasion with many of the past winners and entertainers present, including Yvonne Costello, Kathy Nugent, Helen Jordan, Jimmy Greeley, Ian Dempsey and Billy Brown, as well as Gay Byrne, and Sean Murray of Yoplait. Kevin Healy, head of RTÉ Radio, got the proceedings off on a humorous note with the comment that the competition was now better known as the Kevin Hough Song Contest!

For contestants, the finals of the contest became a really big event when we moved out of Studio 1 at the Radio Centre to the concert venue of Vicar Street in Thomas Street, Dublin. There they had the opportunity to perform before a huge audience as well as on radio. Andy O'Callaghan and his band were with us for all the Vicar Street broadcasts. Andy had great patience and took time and trouble to ensure that everyone was happy with the musical arrangements and the sound and all the equipment. Shelagh Cullen, from the make-up department in RTÉ Television, came on board so that the

Some of the team behind Poparama – *Barry Lang and Ruth Buchanan (presenters), Kevin (producer) and Cathal MacCabe (Controller, RTÉ 2FM)*
(Photo by John Cooney, RTÉ Archives)

young people looked good under lights. The standard was so high that many finalists made a career in music, including Dave Geraghty with the Irish band Bell X1 and recording artist and producer Laura Izibor.

The competition remained extremely popular, and although I moved from 2FM to Radio 1, I produced it for the entirety of its 25-year history. Jean Darling attended every one of the contests in her splendid bonnet. She eventually went to live in Germany with her son but she kept in touch, exchanging cards with Noreen Nichol every Christmas. Jean passed away aged 93 in 2015, but those lovely days with Aunty Poppy will always be remembered.

I was always on the lookout for new ideas to make the *Poparama* programmes on Saturday and Sunday interesting and enjoyable. We had painting and poetry competitions, book reviews, regular contributors on a variety of topics from animals to wild flowers, and listener phone-ins with guest celebrities from showbiz and the sports.

It was quite a coup for us when Gay Byrne agreed to come on the show one Sunday morning – his only day off from his weekly radio programme and *The Late Late Show* on Saturday night. He arrived on the dot of 9 o'clock and gamely answered all the questions our young listeners threw at him, including one that had, no doubt, been prompted by a parent: 'How old are you, Gay?' Without losing a beat he replied, 'I am fifty-three, darling.'

We took him to breakfast at Jurys Hotel, Ballsbridge after the programme. Our super PR lady Mary Crotty was on hand to greet him. Gay was recognised by everyone in the foyer and there was much whispering behind hands and knowing glances. Mary had reserved a quiet corner table, and during the meal Gay amused us with some of his experiences in radio. As the taxi pulled off to take him back home to Howth, I thought what a great man he was to work with.

We got the best from the literary world too. When we ran the Poetry Competition, Eavan Boland generously agreed to be my adjudicator. I drove to her house with boxes of entries and after two weeks she came to our studio to read some of the winning poems. She was so encouraging to our young poets that it became an annual event.

One of our competitions was called the Castlebar Fly In. We asked our listeners to write in saying why they would like a day out at a small airfield. The prize was a train journey to Castlebar with the children's parents, a short flight over Castlebar and out to the Aran Islands, and lunch before returning home. Twelve winners were selected and we had a lovely jaunt to the airfield. It wasn't until they were airborne that I received an anxious phone call from administration in RTÉ enquiring if the children were insured for the flight. I had not even thought of that, but thank goodness it all went off smoothly. Later, Ruth and myself did a loop the loop with one of the pilots. It was thrilling at the time, but disconcerting afterwards when the ground crew joked that that was the way the pilot cured his hangovers; at least, I hope it was a joke. Ruth regretted agreeing to the stunt, saying it was an irresponsible thing to do when she had two children at home. We met the Circuit Court judge Kevin Haugh, who was in Castlebar with his hot air balloon. He told me he was often asked to play the piano at functions by people thinking he was the pianist, so I said that I was often asked to hear cases in court by people thinking I was the judge!

Poparama was broadcast from the 2FM mobile broadcasting unit, the Roadcaster. The same vehicle was used later that year when we returned with the programme for the Castlebar International Song Contest. We chatted with contestants and organisers and heard some of the entries. The following year, 1982, I suggested that Ruth Buchanan co-present the contest with Mike Murphy. The chairman readily agreed and Mike was happy to share the job with an old friend. He and Ruth had both been radio continuity announcers years before in Henry Street. Ruth bought a beautiful dress imprinted with butterflies for the occasion, and we were so proud to see her on national television. Lots of our *Poparama* listeners phoned in to say how beautiful she was.

While we were working in Castlebar we received the news that Sheeba, the all-girl band, had been involved in a horrific car accident. We rushed to the hospital but Maxi was too ill for visitors. Marion Fossett suffered a collapsed lung and Frances Campbell had facial injuries. Maxi's fractured skull required over a hundred stiches and she lost her short-term memory. She spent weeks in hospital and months recuperating at home. It seemed unlikely that Sheeba would ever perform again.

A few weeks after the accident, I got a phone call from Maxi. Although unable to move, she was making plans for the future when she would be up and working again, but at what? She had always loved radio, and DJ Pete Murray once told her that she had a beautiful radio voice. So, here she was on the phone, asking if I thought she could become a presenter. I said it was a brilliant idea. 'But there are very few female broadcasters,' she said, to which I quickly replied, 'There will be one more now.'

I have auditioned many presenters over the years. I featured a slot on 2FM called 'New Voices', on which inexperienced DJs got the chance to present a one-hour programme on a Saturday morning. Many of the applicants sent in demo tapes from their time on pirate radio stations. In the studio we used to spool through the music to the end of the track and listen to the next speech link because we were really only interested in the voice quality. I suggested to Maxi that she put together a programme of speech and short tracks, perhaps describing her travel experiences and playing music from the different countries she had visited. That set her mind buzzing, and she was well prepared when the time came for her to submit her CV and tape. Sheeba did regroup but disbanded a couple of years later, and then Maxi joined 2FM.

On a dreary November evening in 1983, *Drivetime* presenter Jim O'Neill drove me down to the Midlands to do some research. At least that's what I thought. As a programme producer I often had to check on things beforehand. Jim pulled into a large conference centre where there was an award ceremony going on, and only then did he tell me I was to be one of the recipients! The *Tullamore Tribune* had conducted a poll among record companies, pirate radio stations and local papers for its 'Showbiz Awards', and I had been voted Best Radio Producer. That cut glass trophy has pride of place on my coffee table.

One of the many crazy things I did on 2FM was to take to the sky. In association with the Automobile Association, DJ Bob Conway gave live radio traffic reports from a helicopter every weekday morning which covered Dublin city centre, the Liffey Quays, and on out to Stillorgan. I replaced Bob for a few days, and nearly caused mayhem! Each morning at 6.00 am a taxi collected me from the house and brought me out to Weston Airfield, near Lucan. There, I climbed into the cockpit, secured my headphones and contacted the studio to let them know we were ready for lift-off. I had to make reports between 7.00 am and 7.30 am, 8.00 am and 8.30 am, and the last at 8.40 am, but the practicalities of the operation were far from simple. While listening to the pilot with one side of the headphones and hearing the programme with the other, I had to hold a microphone close to speak directly back to the studio above the sound of the engine, and I had to contend with the helicopter swaying and swooping, which often had the effect of dislodging the headphones. Sometimes it was very wet and I couldn't see a thing, so I just made it up! When I got the quays along the Liffey confused one morning,

'Eye in the Sky', 1999
(Photo by Captain John Swan)

a guy called the studio to say, 'Kev got it wrong today. There's no traffic on Arran Quay and he said it was chock-a-block!' My sister Maeve was intrigued by the thought of her brother circling above the city and passing on information. She had just arrived home from Bangkok and turned on the radio to hear me, only to learn that there would be no reports that day owing to fog. That was unavoidable, but I had definitely not covered myself in glory, and was more than happy to hand the mic back to Bob. On my last day in the helicopter I sang a song for the listeners: *I get no kicks from a plane. Flying too high, I'm the Eye in the Sky; it's my idea of nothing to do. But I love it on Radio 2.*

If that was crazy, my next assignment was scary. In 1986 Maxi, who by then was a very popular radio personality with her own show, joined me on a trip overseas. It was Christmastime, and members of the Irish Battalion were serving in the Lebanon as UN peacekeepers. The powers that be in 2FM thought it would be a good idea to support their efforts by making programmes for and about them, and they asked me to produce it. My father was against me going. He knew the Lebanon was in the midst of a civil war and the entire Middle East was a powder keg, but he also knew I was always up for adventure, and with Maxi along as presenter I could not say no. Treasa Davison travelled with us to make a similar programme for Radio 1.

We flew to Heathrow airport with all our equipment, and it was then that things got sticky. Just before our trip a young Irish woman had been tricked into almost carrying a bomb onto an El Al flight, so there was high alert at the airport and the security officials went through our baggage and gear with a fine-tooth comb. I had to open up our Uher recorder and show them that there was nothing concealed in it, play some of the blank tapes to demonstrate that they were indeed tapes, and take out all the batteries for examination. We were questioned in detail and at length about the purpose of our trip, and then re-questioned by another official in case our answers revealed any inconsistencies. When Treasa tried to take a photograph of me being searched, the officials went crazy. The whole procedure took four hours, but afterwards we were allowed onto the British Airways flight for Tel Aviv and happily settled in sumptuous first class.

We were met at the airport by Captain Stephen O'Connor who was to be our driver for the duration and, small world that it is, we discovered he was shortly to be married to the daughter of one of my neighbours at home. Stephen drove us the long journey north across the border and on to the Irish base at Tibnin in south Lebanon. 'Irish Batt' was no cushy number. Conditions were adequate but basic. A week before we arrived, an Irish soldier had been killed by a shot to the head. We were there for six or seven days but the troops had to endure the situation for months on end.

The aim of our programmes was to send messages and greetings from the Irish troops back to their families. We spent the days visiting and recording at all the army outposts. Far from the glitz of stage shows and costumes, there we had to wear flak jackets and helmets as we moved between the various posts, and they were needed. On one occasion, after Maxi and Treasa had retired from exhaustion, I went outside for a bit a fresh air. I suddenly heard footsteps behind me and an armed soldier rushed me back inside, warning me about snipers – it was just not safe to wander about. The next day I met the army chaplain, who turned out to be Father Desmond Campion, a school friend from Synge Street. In a local bar we swapped stories about our old mates and teachers, and inevitably ended up having a singsong with all and sundry.

In the evenings we did what I love to do and do best – entertain. The army had somehow managed to bring a piano over the hills to Tibnin. Hauling a piano around is a great way to put it out of tune, and piano tuners being thin on the ground we had to make do with whatever way it sounded. Maxi and I sang songs from the nineteen sixties and the Hollywood musicals, and in turn we were entertained by some of the fine musicians and singers amongst the Irish troops. Carried away by enthusiasm one night, the lads lifted Maxi clear off the stage and she had to be rescued by some NCOs amid much hilarity.

There is no doubt that South Lebanon was a tough and dangerous station. When we left to return to Tel Aviv there were tears in the eyes of some of those brave soldiers as we

*With Maxi and the Irish UN Peacekeeping troops
in the Lebanon, 1986*

said goodbye. It was a reminder to us of just how much they missed home and family. In Tel Aviv we booked into a good hotel, had proper showers, put on the glad rags and hit the town to dance long into the night. Maxi is a fine singer and presenter, but, more than that, she is one of my oldest and dearest friends. She worked on documentaries and on television, and her honeyed voice and personal warmth kept listeners company through the wee small hours on RTÉ Radio 1's *Late Date* for eleven years, and helped people to greet the day with *Risin' Time* for a further eleven years before she retired in 2015. I will never forget sharing an army tank with Maxi – only she could look fetching in a blue UN helmet.

Chapter 8

Oh Yes He Is … Oh No He Isn't

I have always got a buzz from combining my day job with the exhilarating world of show business, in all its great variety. In 1979, RTÉ presenter Donncha O Dulaing approached me at work to ask if I would direct a concert at the Carlton Cinema in Dublin. I jumped at the chance, particularly when I heard the line-up: The Wolfe Tones, violinist Geraldine O'Grady and actress Anna Manahan, Irish dancers and a harpist, with Donncha as the MC. The artists were on top form, the Wolfe Tones would have packed houses anywhere, and the whole evening gave me the confidence to do something I had always wanted to do – produce my own concerts.

A couple of years later a suitable occasion presented itself quite naturally. I was distressed to learn that my dear friend Veronica Dunne was going through a rough time with the breakup of her marriage, and I thought of gathering a few of her closest friends together and building a small concert around her. Ronnie doubted whether she would be in any fit state to appear in public but, after some persuading, she agreed to do it. On 8 December 1978, Veronica Dunne, Geraldine O'Grady, pianist Havelock Nelson and compère

96

Valerie McGovern took to the stage of the Royal Dublin Society with a programme of light classical music. The event was a sell-out, and audience reaction to all the performers was rapturous. Ronnie was greatly heartened, and Kevin Hough Productions was launched.

I can never resist taking to the boards myself, however. I had seen a great production of Harry Tierney's *Irene* at the Adelphi Theatre in London with Jon Pertwee playing Madame Lucy, the flamboyant couturier for whom Irene models. I knew it was a part I would relish – the comedy, the clothes, the hit song 'They Go Wild, Simply Wild, Over Me', and when the O'Connell Musical Society offered me the part in 1979, I was thrilled. Cathal MacCabe produced and Helen Jordan was Irene. Helen and I had already performed together in *Showboat* with the Navan Musical Society (where my sister Ursula had been leader of the orchestra), so it was a really good experience. We went simply wildly over the top and had a riotous time, much to the startled enjoyment of the good people of Killester in north Dublin. That production is remembered even now on the O'Connell Musical Society's website: 'to say that it was lively is an understatement'.

Suddenly it was 1981 and I was 37. Normally I would not pay much attention to my age but when the Thurles Musical Society came knocking on my door for me to play the aged scoundrel Fagin in *Oliver!* I took a look at myself in the mirror and thought I was too young, really, but what a part. Evelyn Lunny of the RTÉ makeup department was convinced she could put years on me, and I took myself down to Bourke's on Dame Street for suitably threadbare attire. They came up with a wonderful costume that had been worn by John Molloy in the Olympia Theatre production. Before the first show, I was

Fagin in Oliver! *1981*

chuffed to receive a telegram from Brendan Grace wishing me luck and signing it 'Your Co-Star'. As the lights dimmed the magic of theatre wove its spell and I became that devious and ancient character.

> *'A man's got a heart, hasn't he? Joking apart – hasn't he? And tho' I'd be the first one to say that I wasn't a saint, I'm finding it hard to be really as black as they paint.'*

As a guest performer for a country musical society, you always feel that the locals are watching your every move, whether that is true or not. So after each performance in Thurles, I went back to my hotel room. Some of the cast thought I was being a bit uppity and was not a good mixer. I had to explain that the role was demanding and that if I partied every night my voice might give out. They accepted that, but warned me that I would have to show my true colours when it was all over. So after the last night, I was well up for the party – I had to make up for all that lost time. Make up I did, and we were seen leaving the party for bed at 5.30 the next morning. Did I have a head when I woke up? Yes, I did.

Back at the day job, *Poparama* was still one of my major programmes, and I was delighted when Brendan Grace, comedian and singer, agreed to come in and have a chat on the show in 1981. Brendan was not only famous for having been with the Gingermen band and for writing his big hit of 1975 'Combine Harvester', but it seemed that half of Ireland loved his comedic schoolboy creation 'Bottler'. All the children wanted to talk to Bottler on the phone. Some of them told him their jokes and we gave away tickets to Brendan's next performance and of course played his songs.

After the programme we went to the canteen for a cuppa. As we chatted, Brendan mentioned that he was going into the Olympia Theatre with a pantomime, *Bottler and the Beanstalk*, to be directed by Bil Keating from RTÉ. He knew I had been in several pantos with Jack Cruise, and wondered if I would play the role of the Demon King. Having checked to make sure I could combine my work with the performances I was happy to accept. Eileen Reid (who had been with the showband Eileen Reid and the Cadets) was principal boy, and Jacinta Whyte was principal girl. Corinne Kennedy, a great friend of mine, played Fairy Queen and Chris Casey was the Dame.

As the mean old Demon King I got a mean old song to sing: '*I'm wicked, totally wicked. I'm as wicked and as horrible as can be*', and how the children hissed and booed! I loved every minute of it and Brendan was a knockout with the audience.

The Demon King in Bottler and the Beanstalk, *1982*

In 1983, Bil Keating asked me to appear on the *Brendan Grace Show* on RTÉ television. I always had a bit of a vocation but I never thought I would end up as a nun with Brendan Grace as my sister nun, beard and all. Having spent years on the stage, being in front of the camera was a new experience for me. The series lasted for eight weeks and if the audience got half the fun out of it that we did, then they must have been falling out of their chairs laughing. The scripts had been written for the action to take place at outside locations, but money was scarce, so instead we were in the studio doing such mad things as riding a motorbike or pretending to fish, with added sound-effects to suggest the great outdoors.

We kept up our act as nuns for a summer season at the Gaiety. For once we had a scorcher of a summer that year, and that's always bad for theatre because people just flock to the beach. To promote the show, Brendan and I appeared on *The Late Late* in our nuns' get-up. I was called Sister Kawasaki and he was Sister Hairy O'Meara and we told a few jokes. Another day we rode the motorbike into Dublin and it was so funny to watch people in buses and at traffic lights doing double-takes at the two nuns astride. We decided to have a pint in Davy Byrne's Pub on Duke Street and Brendan went to the Gents, still in the habit, and all the men dashed out in various states of undress, horrified by the appearance of a hairy nun in their midst. When we had stopped laughing we rode down Moore Street and handed out complimentary theatre tickets to some of the dealers.

Getting into bad habits with Brendan on RTÉ's
Brendan Grace Show, *1983*

That same year Brendan hosted a series of variety shows, *Sunday Night at the Gaiety*, which was a bit like ITV's *The London Palladium Show*, with guest acts from different countries. I was a regular on the show, as were the girl band Sheeba and musical director Noel Kelehan.

The show was performed live in a fully functioning theatre, so the RTÉ television crew had to move in straight after the regular show finished on a Saturday night to have all the sets and technical equipment ready for our rehearsal on the Sunday afternoon. They worked through the night but they did not mind – they said they were on 'golden time'. While the overtime bill may have been high, so too were the audience figures. We got fantastic ratings. When the show moved from the Gaiety to the Olympia it was just as

Stepping it out with Brendan on
Sunday Night at the Gaiety, *1983*

popular. I often think it would be great to see a variety show special televised from the Abbey Theatre, but I suppose the cost would be prohibitive.

Working with Brendan was a bit unpredictable. Although most performances were a breeze, one night he gave me a bad fright. We were supposed to be opening the show together as the two nuns, but by five minutes to eight Brendan had not appeared. Everyone backstage was on tenterhooks, fearing I would have to go on by myself. He swept in almost as the curtain was rising, and I nearly collapsed with relief. After the show I told him how worried we had been, and he said he had not understood the significance of the half-hour call. Brendan was used to performing with a band and later travelling the country in his road bus, so he had treated the Gaiety show as just another gig. I explained that there are rules of the house when it comes to theatre and one of them is that the performers are ready well ahead of time. He never put us through that particular agony again, although there were others. On stage, I never knew what he was going to come out with next. I always played the straight man to both Jack Cruise and to Brendan – the guy who fed them the lines so that they could come out with the killer quips. Jack usually stuck to the script, but with Brendan I had to fly by the seat of my pants!

After the Gaiety we transferred to the Cork Opera House. It became a two-man show without the services of Sheeba and Noel Kelehan, but with the excellent Second City Jazz Band from Cork. I played piano to cover costume changes for Brendan, and Vera Patterson from Wardrobe in RTÉ ensured that all the clothes were to hand because we each had to make rapid changes in the wings. The weather was still hot and some of the houses were poor. It was great to see my cousins from the farm in Monagea there to support us, and, as word spread, we got better attendances and enjoyed the run. On our return to Dublin we immediately began to make plans for the next Christmas pantomime.

Bottler Crusoe opened at the end of December 1983 in the Olympia. It was billed as a 'spectacular family pantomime' with a 'star-studded cast'. It featured Brendan as Bottler, with Val Fitzpatrick (who also directed) as the Dame, and Helen Jordan, Joe Cahill, Cecil Nash and George Henry. I was Mincemeat, the baddie. Although it was a good run, it was not as popular as some of the Jack Cruise pantos had been.

The next year I moved up from playing the baddie to playing the dame in Brendan's panto, *Bottler in Nipperland*. Directed by Cathal MacCabe, the show was a huge success. It toured Ireland to packed houses and extended runs. Yvonne Costello was a very sexy Fairy Queen and Jacinta Whyte was principal girl. The Billie Barry Kids were just great, and a very young Angeline Ball was a member of the chorus; even then it was obvious she had terrific potential. It was wonderful to see her later as Imelda Quirke in the film *The Commitments*, with my nephew Félim Gormley (Ursula's son) as saxophonist Dean Fay, and then in *Doc Martin* on UTV. She is one talented lady.

I did pantos, TV and stage shows with Brendan and it was always a pleasure to work with him; the laughs we had. Nowadays he tours occasionally and is as popular as ever with Dublin audiences, but he spends most of his time at home in Florida. Brendan is blessed with a lovely voice and has recorded many songs, including 'The Dutchman'; I still get a lump in my throat whenever I hear it.

Chapter 9

Come On-A My House

With the turning of yet another year I knew I would have to focus on getting a place of my own. It was 1984, and for forty years I had enjoyed living with my family, first at Beechwood Avenue, and then at Meadow Close, Dundrum. Michael and five of the girls had married and left, but Fionnuala and myself had stayed with our parents.

I loved entertaining. Many of my friends from RTÉ and the showbiz world would come to the house for a night of music, especially after a show, and my parents liked nothing better than a chat with them before heading to bed. But as we talked and sang into the small hours I was always aware that they were upstairs trying to sleep.

The time had come for me to move on. I searched and searched for something that would suit me. Location was important for getting into RTÉ and around Dublin for the shows, but I had a limited budget. I really wanted a bungalow and it had to be detached so that I could play my piano at any time of the day and night without disturbing my neighbours. I was almost in despair when Ejvind Mogensen, my

105

sister Maeve's Danish husband, told me of a little house on Whitehall Road in Churchtown that had just gone on sale.

I went to have a look. The sight that confronted me was not promising. It was a dilapidated cottage with attached garage, shrouded in trees and undergrowth. Inside, the rooms were pokey and dark and smelt of damp. There was no kitchen, just a sort of pantry. Then I glanced out at the garden. It was big, wild and romantic and right beside the grounds of a golf course. When I stepped into it I could have been in the depths of the country. No road noise, just the sound of birds high in the trees. There and then I fell in love. I knew that I could make the house my home and be happy living there.

Joan La Grue came to view the property with me. Joan and I have been friends since the late 1960s. I introduced her to Veronica Dunne, with whom she trained before joining the R&R. Now she sings at concerts and with the University Church Choir and is one of the most popular people I know, always attending garden parties, lunches, dinners; and she shops like no one else. We sometimes go shopping together and she advises me on what to wear, so with imagination like that, I knew she was the right person to tell me if I was being completely crazy about the house. I was so glad when she saw the way it could be and gave it the thumbs-up. Joan knew I was anxious about incurring heavy expenses with a bridging loan, and she asked a pal of hers in the Irish Permanent Building Society if he could rush my mortgage through, which he did. Before long, I was settled in my very own house, lighting fires in all the rooms to keep down the damp, and wrapping up warm against the drafts from the rotten windows and the breeze billowing under the floorboards from the garage. So, while not exactly snug as a bug, I was delighted with myself.

Family and friends pitched in with furniture and offers of cleaning and painting. I hired five burly gardeners to clear out the worst of the jungle and cut down trees to let in the light, and then my father got to work. Whenever I came home from work he would invariably be out in the garden, getting it into shape. He loved doing that, and I loved the results. Nearly all my family are keen gardeners, but green fingers I have not. That garden is still my oasis at the end of the day, and when one of my sisters arrives up with a pot of scarlet geraniums or a fuchsia bush, it is a joy.

Shortly after moving in, I had a stroke of luck when the government set up a grant scheme for new kitchens. It was just the incentive I needed. I had an extension built for a kitchen and breakfast room with windows overlooking the garden. It was so cosy. Not only could I cook and eat, I could work at the table in space, light and warmth.

You may be wondering about my family and where they were with their lives. My parents had retired in 1974 and sold the shop on the Crumlin Road. We left the house on Beechwood Avenue and moved to Meadow Close in Dundrum. Once there, Dad used every inch of the small garden for fruit and vegetables. There was a plum and an apple tree, and he planted tomatoes, carrots, potatoes, lettuce, scallions, onions and rhubarb. Dad outgrew that space fairly soon and rented a plot from the county council for yet more vegetables. When he was not gardening in his own house, he was gardening in mine. My sister Patricia took to gardening in a big way and to this day grows lots of vegetables for her family.

The first day of February 1986 was one day that will never be forgotten in our family. We all got decked out in our best bib and tucker for the wedding of my sister Ursula's

*Triple celebration: mother Patricia, niece Gráinne
and sister Ursula. 1986 (Photo by Frank McGrath Junior)*

daughter, Gráinne, in Dublin's University Church. The day
was so special, it even made headlines in the *Irish Independent*: 'The wedding date with a familiar ring'.

My mother and father were married on 1 February 1936.
On the same day 25 years later Ursula married Frank Gormley, and 25 years after that Gráinne married Curtis Adler
from Wisconsin. So it was a triple celebration – a wedding
for the Adlers, a silver anniversary for the Gormleys and a
golden anniversary for the Houghs. Just look at them there in
that photograph – my mother, my niece and my sister. Such
happy times.

There were always visitors at Meadow Close. Mam and
Dad were so hospitable and loved seeing the family. In 1986
Fionnuala was living in Leeds, where she was a member of

English National Opera North. Michael was married and had a house in Castleknock and a shop in Dunshaughlin. My sisters Ursula, Maura, Phil and Patricia and their families often came over, and Maeve and Ejvind joined them whenever they were not travelling the world. My home in Churchtown was near Dundrum and I was in and out of the house all the time. On a Saturday night you would often find Mam's brothers and sisters over for a game of cards and a chat.

My parents did everything together and were very much part of the community in Dundrum. They sang in the local church choir until well into their late seventies. Dad delivered food baskets for St Vincent de Paul and distributed meals on wheels, stopping that only when he was in his early eighties because his driving was not so good anymore. Just two short years after that wedding photograph was taken Mam was diagnosed with cancer. We installed a stair lift in the house; stairs can be such a pain when one gets old. In 1989 Mam became very ill and spent weeks in hospital before moving into Patricia's home. We knew she didn't have long and contacted Maeve, who was living in Bangkok. Thank God she arrived just before Mam died. We were broken-hearted. At the funeral Maura, one of her sisters, said to me, 'Kev, we will never play Scrabble again'.

Without Mam, Dad went downhill very quickly. I was worried about him driving over to my house because he was on medication for angina, but then he gave up his car and handed it on to Patricia. I missed him coming every other day to work on the garden, and I missed seeing him on the seat by the big spruce tree where I would join him for a cuppa.

Dad was taken bad with his breathing one day and I brought him to hospital. We all visited regularly, and I always called in before I went to play piano at Shannon's Restaurant in Stillorgan. He liked doing the Lotto. I brought him a scratch card every night, so I was the last to see him. I got a message around 2.30 am to say he had passed away and to bring in the family. I made all the calls, and we gathered at the hospital. Maeve flew in from Bangkok and his coffin was opened for her to say goodbye. It was just eleven months after our mother had died.

They were both such a huge part of our lives. They attended every show we appeared in and Mam was always at the Feis competitions when we sang or played. She taught us how to cook, run a house, look after one another and make the best of things. Through all the years of our childhood and on into adulthood, Mam and Dad encouraged us in everything we did. How blessed we were to have such wonderful parents.

A couple of years after moving into my house I came home to a scene of devastation. The place had been burgled, and wrecked in the process. All the usual things were stolen – music centre, television, LPs, furniture, even a white leather jacket that had once belonged to Phil Lynott. The thieves had gained easy access through one of the rotten windows, so there was no point trying to recover from this blow before I got new windows fitted all round and an alarm system installed.

But recover I did, and over the next few years I had more work done. I wanted a party pad with space to entertain my friends, a place for my piano, walls for my photographs. What I did not expect was that my home improvements would become frontline news. 'Knock a bit here, add a bit there and

Kevin's bungalow is bliss' was the eye-catching feature in the *Irish Press* in February 1991, and later mentioned on the airways! Ejvind had suggested that I go for an open-plan look, so I had the two small living areas connected by knocking through and creating arches on either side of the fireplace. The wall between the living room and the terrible garage was demolished, and a beautiful new extension erected with a sloping pine ceiling and skylights to flood it with light. Ejvind designed a bar area, and by chance I had these plans in my music case at the Castlebar Song Contest (perhaps not by chance, I pored over them all the time). There I met Liam Wylie, a bass player in the RTÉ Concert Orchestra, who told me he was also a carpenter. He took a look at the bar design and said he could make it. He was as good as his word, so good, in fact, that I also got him to make a unit for the television/music centre, a coffee table, a cabinet for the bathroom and storage for my CD and record collection. Liam had such a talent for wood, but he was also a brilliant musician. I met him a while ago and asked if he was still making cabinets but he said he was too busy with the orchestra.

All the work was done. It was party time! I borrowed a huge barbeque from Mark Shannon and, as the meat was sizzling, more and more friends and family arrived. It made my heart swell to see people greeting each other, chatting and laughing in the garden, moving with ease through the house, and as each one came in there were exclamations of surprise and admiration. 'Jaysus,' shrieked Twink, 'this place is Hollywood!' Ronnie Dunne, Yvonne Costello, Eileen Reid, Billy Brown, Susan Hamilton, Noel O'Shea, Maxi, Cathal MacCabe, Ian Dempsey, my family – there were over 50 guests, and the house and garden embraced them all.

Noel O'Shea, my tree surgeon friend, is renowned as a psychic and people were queuing up to have their palms read. Twink and himself disappeared into a room and twenty minutes later we were wondering what in the name of God was going on. He had a lot to tell her, obviously, and we still laugh about it.

With all those extraordinary singers gathered in one place, it was not long before the piano lid was opened and I was glad the roof had been checked because otherwise it would have blown right off! We partied until five in the morning. The house had done me proud.

Chapter 10

More Than a Couple of Swells

I had been thinking for some time that my period with 2FM was drawing to a natural close. The station was well established and there were plenty of bright young people to bring it forward. The *Poparama* show was ending, and the song contest had secured a new sponsor. So, without much fuss in the late 1980s, I changed stations and moved back to RTÉ Radio 1 or, as Brendan Balfe liked to call it, 'The Senior Service'. And I was so glad I did, because I got to work on some wonderful shows.

My first programme on my return as producer was *Words and Music*. It was a well-worn radio formula where a notable person talks about their life and chooses five or six records. Over the years such people as Garry Hynes, Bronwyn Conroy, Brendan Kennelly, Nuala O'Faolain, Cyril Cusack, Kate O'Toole and Dan Treston appeared on the show. The presenter was John Skehan, and what a contrast there was between him and the young DJs on 2FM. John had been an army officer and was a senior announcer when Radio Éireann broadcast from Henry Street. You could not mistake his deep chestnut voice for anyone else's, but despite his serious tone,

John could be quite light-hearted and was good at getting guests to open up. John had retired but came back especially to present *Words and Music*. We travelled all around Ireland and to London and New York for the show.

In New York John interviewed the Hollywood actress Geraldine Fitzgerald. After the recording Geraldine invited us back for drinks to the penthouse she owned with her banker husband. It was a magnificent apartment, but quite terrifying because everything in it – the walls, sofas and carpets – was white. As my assistant Pauline O'Donnell sipped her red wine I had visions of it spilling and ruining the perfect scenario, but she was far too careful for that; we were all careful. Geraldine told us stories about some of the films she had been in. She played Isabella Linton in *Wuthering Heights* in 1939. During filming, Laurence Olivier was out of sorts with everyone, including the director William Wyler and his leading lady Merle Oberon, because he had wanted Vivien Leigh to play Cathy. David Niven (as Edgar Linton) refused to cry when Cathy died, saying it was not in his contract to cry. After much argument, he agreed to bury his head in an eiderdown so that the audience would assume he was distraught. There was another difficulty on the 1946 movie *O.S.S.* Geraldine and Alan Ladd were two American spies on a mission in Nazi-occupied France who fell in love, but all their scenes together had to be conducted while Alan stood on a box because he was so short.

Sadly, John Skehan died in November 1992. Mary Kennedy took over and she, too, proved to be an excellent presenter. By that time I was also working on *Theatre Nights*, first as producer and then as presenter/producer. The premise of *Theatre Nights* was to publicise events that the

Association of Irish Musical Societies (AIMS) were organising throughout the country, and to record snippets from the shows and talk to the participants. During the summer season, when there was not much on, we extended our remit to cover professional shows in Ireland and in London, and to review productions that might interest those travelling to Britain. Well! That suited me just swell, and I had a fine time in Ireland and the West End and farther afield, and got to meet some fascinating people.

One of my first trips away as presenter was in 1991 when I went to London to interview producer David Puttnam and the actress Glenn Close, who were launching their film *Meeting Venus*. I travelled with Mary McGoris, then working for the *Irish Independent*. David Puttnam was friendly and courteous during my pre-arranged, 20-minute interview, and he gave me enough material about his career to make a good programme. His ever-present manager ensured that the time allocation was strictly adhered to, which was fair enough considering it was one of David's many interviews that day.

Journalists who were invited to lunch with Glenn Close and the other stars were allowed to ask questions during dessert. On our way to the restaurant we were asked not to mention the break-up of Glenn's marriage because she was still upset about it. We found Glenn to be very approachable and open to all sorts of questions. In *Meeting Venus* she played the part of a Swedish opera singer, with her singing voice dubbed by Kiri Te Kanawa. When asked whether she herself could sing, Glenn immediately stood up and sang out a scale for us (I recently heard her in *Sunset Boulevard* and she has a good voice, though not an operatic one). An American journalist was sitting beside me. As the session progressed I knew she was itching to ask about the break-up, and, as bold as brass, she piped up, 'Tell us, Glenn, why did your relationship not last?' Glenn's manager interjected by saying that Miss Close would not discuss that today, and the American subsided back into her chair. Before leaving for the airport the PR lady, Mary Crotty, swept Mary McGoris and myself off to afternoon tea at Harrods.

As well as *Theatre Nights*, I also recorded occasional shows for the Radio 1 *In Concert* series. Daniel O'Donnell was putting on a big show in Limerick, so I went along, and discovered some of my relatives from Monagea, Newcastle West and Ballingarry were there to see him. I called into Daniel's dressing room with my sound engineer. His table was covered with tablets and lotions. 'Kev', he said. 'I don't think I can go on tonight. I have a really bad sore throat.' I told him my family had come from all over the county (never mind the rest of the audience), so could he please do his best? He did, and as usual he went down a storm. After the show he spent an hour signing autographs and my relatives were ecstatic! At my B&B the next morning I met some of Daniel's fans. They were following his tour, town by town, and though they knew his whole programme, it did not matter; they just could not wait to hear him again. Now that is loyalty. My housekeeper, Mrs Foley, loved Daniel, and when I managed to get tickets for her a few times, I was really in her good books.

One of my career highlights was the recording of Shirley Bassey at the Point Depot, Dublin in 1992. Her manager came to see me before the show to remind me that it was Shirley's name on the ticket, so it was important to keep the band in the background. My sound engineer was Paddy McBreen and he was super.

On stage, Shirley not only looked amazing, but with a few glances and swaggers she had the audience eating out of her hand. After 'Big Spender', she looked straight at them and said, 'Not bad for a granny, eh?', and she brought the house down with 'Goldfinger'. But it was not just her singing. She had a musical director who was one of the best I have ever come across. He never took his eyes off her and made sure everything was perfect. Her gowns that night were really striking and I learned that they had all been made by an Irish lady. Shirley Bassey is one of those stars that thoroughly deserve the title 'Dame', awarded to her in 2000.

In 1995 one of the big stage hits in the West End was *Jolson* at the Victoria Palace Theatre. The unlikely star was comedian Brian Conley, whose performance was so convincing that every night the audiences responded to him as if he were Al Jolson himself. My pal John Conroy received stunning reviews as Jolson's sardonic dresser, Frankie Holmes. I arranged an interview with Brian for *Theatre Nights* and, reading up on him beforehand, I discovered that he was big into tattoos and that he had one on his backside. During our chat we went through the usual things about his childhood and how he got started in show business. I eventually mentioned the rumour about the tattoo. There and then he dropped his trousers and on his buttocks were inscribed the words 'NO ENTRY'. I told him it was the first time I had ever had a bum on radio and he thought that was hilariously funny.

Theatre Nights received an invitation in 1996 to attend the first ever Musical of the Year Competition in Denmark's second city, Aarhus. I was promised interviews with Julia McKenzie, Bonnie Langford, John Barrowman and anyone else I could collar. I travelled with actor and broadcaster

Máire Nic Gearailt. Groups from all over Europe performed excerpts from new musicals. The delightful Bonnie Langford was in one of these and I met up with her afterwards. She was glad to talk and get publicity for her forthcoming production of *Sweet Charity* at London's Victoria Palace Theatre. She had always wanted to play Charity but no one had asked her, so she intended to mount the show herself, using her own house as financial collateral! I went to see the show two years later and was so disappointed for Bonnie. It was not well cast or received and I believe she lost a lot of money.

At the finale of the Musical of the Year, there was a grand concert and prize-giving ceremony presented by Sir Peter Ustinov. He used an auto cue throughout because it was going out live on Danish television. He was 75 then and I felt it was a huge effort for him. One of the judges was Björn Ulvaeus from ABBA, co-composer of such musicals as *Chess* and *Mama Mia!* After the concert I talked with the theatre critic Jack Tinker, who told me he had once single-handedly closed a show in London called *The Fields of Ambrosia*. When I enquired why he had given it such a scathing review, he said, 'Well, the best song contained the line, "We are in the fields of Ambrosia where nobody knows you," and it went downhill after that!' I also caught up with the Scottish/American actor John Barrowman, who had been on *Theatre Nights* when he starred in *Sunset Boulevard* in London, and we had a great conversation.

My conversation with Julia McKenzie was a different kettle of fish. I had seen her in *Side by Side by Sondheim* with Millicent Martin in the West End and was excited to be getting the chance of doing a special *Theatre Nights* about her. However, when we met I knew I was in for a difficult time.

She had a long face on her and signed her contract for the interview fee with very bad grace. She then gave me so little information about her career that I later had to pad out my show with music from the few productions she had been in. Perhaps I caught her on a bad day – it can happen to the best of us – but her attitude was disappointing. Putting that experience aside, Máire and I had an enjoyable few days, and I came home with the makings of some good programmes.

One of my most memorable programmes was recorded behind prison bars! The news that *West Side Story* was going to be staged in Mountjoy Prison in November 1996 was all over the airways and the papers. As it was going to take place in the main exercise yard of the prison with tickets for the five performances on sale to the general public, it was even debated in the Dáil, where concerns were raised over security. The Mountjoy Prison Players had previously put on productions for friends and family and a few invited guests, but this show was going to be run in conjunction with Pimlico Opera from Britain and a team of professional singers. Its musical director, Wasfi Kani, founded the company in 1987, with the aim of using music and drama to encourage personal development through participation, particularly among young and disadvantaged people. Pimlico brings opera to the people in unusual places – hospitals, banks, country houses – and had already performed with the inmates of several British prisons.

What a great production to get for *Theatre Nights*. I contacted John Lonergan, Governor of Mountjoy, and requested interviews with him and the inmate cast members, and permission to record the show. John was all in favour, and after he got government approval we went ahead.

On a very cold day in October I found myself approaching the huge wooden doors of the prison with some trepidation. Once inside, I did not much like it when gates were banged shut behind me, but on my way to the Governor's office I saw a lovely tray of hot buns being brought to the inmates for their afternoon tea and I thought maybe this is not the worst place to be on a day like today. John was a friendly, forthright man, and during our interview he spoke of those in his charge with great compassion. He believed there was good in everyone, and he hoped that people could leave his institution better equipped for the outside world than when they had entered. He had initiated programmes in education, crafts, the learning of new skills and, of course, drama. I had a list of cast members to interview, some of whom were women from the Dóchas Centre on the prison campus.

An officer was assigned to me for the afternoon to ensure that all went smoothly. He brought me to a cell where I set up my tape recorder. I was to see each person on his or her own, but he said he would stand guard outside the door. He pointed to a bell on the wall that I should push if anyone attacked me.

As I talked with the young men and women, I gained some understanding of why they had ended up in there. I heard stories about their challenging circumstances and listened to regrets for the crimes they had committed. Most had a release date and plans for a better future, such as working with special needs children or using their newfound skills in the building trade. They were all buzzing about their performances; some were so talented, they were taking the minor leads. One of the guys said that he was so high about being in the show that he hadn't taken drugs for weeks. Another one told me about being hopelessly hooked on heroin, which had led to him robbing banks. 'I grew up with ten people. Six are dead of AIDS and three are waiting to die. I've been tested and they won't say if I've got it or not.' A young woman, a talented actor, was due to be let out in December, and all she wanted was to be at home with her family (John Lonergan invited me to a play in the prison the following year, and I was dismayed to see the same woman on the stage again, back inside).

On 15 November, each member of the audience was checked through security, and every seat in the covered and heated yard was filled. After four weeks of rehearsals, the professional cast and the inmates took to the stage, and it made international news. 'In Irish Jail, Jets and Sharks Rumble Again' was the headline for an article in *The New York Times* (dated 18 November 1996), which stated that 'The inmates, wielding floppy rubber knives and just barely pulling their punches in rumbles, were performing *West Side Story*, currently the hottest political and theatrical ticket in Dublin.' It was an instant hit, and all five nights were sold out. As for security, the audience were asked to remain seated after the performance while the stars of the show were escorted back to their cells.

I recorded the Gala Night performance on 18 November with a crew of four from RTÉ's Outside Broadcasting Unit. President Mary Robinson, American Ambassador Jean Kennedy Smith, government ministers and even James Bond himself, Pierce Brosnan, were among the guests for an electrifying show. It received amazing publicity. Most newspapers mentioned that I would be featuring highlights of the musical on *Theatre Nights*, and the phones started hopping in the press office with listeners incensed that I should give airtime to criminals. But I can tell you that I loved talking with those young people, some of whom came from the most deprived backgrounds, and I actually felt sad leaving them.

Back in the studio I had such good material that I decided to devote one programme to each of the two acts. I interspersed the interviews between the music and it worked like a dream. I am told that every transistor radio in Mountjoy was tuned in to hear their show on both Sundays. On 'the outside', too, people found the programmes compelling and I got great feedback. One of the touching letters I received was from a father thanking me for interviewing his son, who had played a Jet. He felt so proud of the boy, and couldn't wait to see him on his release.

Siân Phillips, the wonderful Welsh actress, made a deep impression on me. In 1997 I attended *Marlene,* her one-woman show at the Lyric Theatre on Shaftesbury Avenue in London. Siân was dazzling, especially when she sang 'Falling in Love Again' wearing 'the dress' – a replica of the iconic Jean-Louis designed garment, flesh-coloured and skin-tight that moved with her like a glittering waterfall of diamonds. Apparently it took four people seven weeks to bead and had cost a fortune. I was lucky enough to see Marlene Dietrich herself in the original dress in the Adelphi Cinema, Dublin in the 1960s. Even then there was an aura surrounding it, and it was always kept under wraps until the performance. My Aunt Joan was wardrobe mistress at RTÉ when Marlene made a television appearance there, and she got a peek at the dress. The original was rubber-backed and encrusted with rhinestones, and the slit up the side went on for ever to show off those amazing legs. Siân revelled in the part of Marlene, and she was generous enough to grant me an interview for *Theatre Nights.* We spoke of her life and career, and she was pleased when I mentioned that I thought she was superb in *A Little Night Music* with Judi Dench in 1995. She did not want to talk about her marriage to Peter O'Toole, other than to say her own acting had had to take a very back seat when she went with him to far-flung hot and humid places, especially when he was working on *Lawrence of Arabia*. But she now lived very happily in a flat in Kensington with two Burmese cats, and was able to concentrate on her own projects again. She was, and is, so charming and beautiful, and what a great artist.

I have always enjoyed working in Cork, particularly in the Everyman Palace Theatre on MacCurtain Street, which is a little Victorian gem. To celebrate its one hundred years of music, dance and comedy, the theatre underwent a refurbishment in 1997, and then threw a birthday party in the form of a gala concert. Since I was presenting *Theatre Nights* at the time, they requested a recording of the event and invited me to act as MC. Cathal MacCabe directed the show, and top of the bill was soprano Kathleen Tynan and comedian Niall Tóibín. During our two days of rehearsals, I got a chance to talk with Niall. I reminded him of taking part in the radio plays my uncle Patrick McNulty had written for children, some of which involved animals that had to be impersonated by the actors. He laughed as we remembered his remark when he came into studio one day and caught sight of the script: 'Not a fucking duck again this week!'

After the concert, I went to the bar for a quiet drink, but a local lady bore down on me to say, 'Was there no one here in Cork to do that job as MC? Sure, it would have saved you coming all the way from Dublin.' I looked her straight in the eye and said, 'Madam, there was no one good enough!' She took to her heels and I was able to enjoy my drink in peace.

As a small boy, I was mesmerised by the magic of panto-mime – I am sure it is one of the reasons I became hooked on theatre – and the two people who epitomised pantomime for thousands of children were Jimmy O'Dea and Maureen Potter. Over the years I saw Maureen perform many times and marvelled at her skill and timing as an actress and a co-medienne. Her monologues on the dreaded Irish mammy were nothing short of genius. With all my experience organ-ising talent contests, one in particular rings all too true. The mammy is in the front row urging on her young one, Christy, who is up on stage in his first Irish dancing competition.

> *'Go on, Criostor, lift them legs! Don't kick the judge! Here! Stop a minute – his shoelaces is open. Wha d'ya mean, Judge, he's disqualified? Sure, he never got started. Are ya blind? Can ya not see he has the makins of a national champeen?'*

In 1998 Bill O'Donovan of Radio 1 asked me if I would produce an eight-part series on Maureen for radio, because there was not enough material stored in the archives. I met Maureen and her husband, scriptwriter Jack O'Leary, to dis-cuss the programme. The series, *Maureen Potter Looks Back*, was presented by Maureen herself, and she chose pieces of music to highlight her reminiscences. We recorded one pro-gramme a week in the studio, and as she read out her script, she and Jack would sometimes make changes to it, and if they thought a different disc would be better, I ran down to the gram library to get it. With more than sixty years as an enter-tainer – she began at the age of ten – Maureen had a bagful of memories to share, and she told them with such humour and honesty that we pulled in a large audience and the series was a huge success. She spoke about her early life, her first broadcast for Radio Éireann in 1935 and her touring days in England as a youngster. Her long-running radio series, *The Maureen Potter Show*, was written by Jack O'Leary, as were many of the sketches in more than fifty pantomimes in the Gaiety and the *Gaels of Laughter* show that packed the theatre for eighteen

Maureen Potter Looks Back, *1998*

summer seasons. She also spoke about her roles as a straight actress in plays by O'Casey, Beckett, Shaw and Sheridan.

Maureen had a prodigious memory. She was renowned in pantomime for asking the names of birthday children in the audience. She would memorise these at the interval and then mention them at the line-up before the curtain fell. Her record was 67. A lot of happy children next day told their friends that Maureen Potter had called out their names from the stage. She would try to set a good example to the children by drinking lots of milk, only hers was laced with whiskey!

One of the stories Maureen told me was that, shortly after returning from a tour of England with the Jack Hylton Band, she was walking to rehearsals for a panto with Jimmy O'Dea and an oul wan shouted across the street, 'Will ya look at that Potter wan with the dark glasses – does she think she's a star or somethin'!' Maureen had a bad eye infection at the time, caused by the musty books she bought in second-hand shops everywhere she went. She was always reading, even in rehearsals, and whenever she came home from touring, she would have a huge box of books with her. I loved working with Maureen. When the series finished she sent the most beautiful arrangement of flowers to my house that lasted for months.

Maureen suffered from crippling arthritis, but that did not stop her from working. A few years after those programmes I was thrilled when she agreed to adjudicate for me with the Docklands Senior Citizens Talent Showcase. Her final appearance for that contest in the NCH was in 2004, and my last sight of her was of being lifted into a taxi after the show. Maureen died later that year.

International stars were always a feature on *Theatre Nights*, but it was the local Irish scene that formed the backbone of the show, and people like Louise Studley. Louise was a leading lady for the Rathmines and Rathgar Musical Society for many years; if she had chosen to emigrate she would have been a huge star in the West End. We chatted about her roles and favourite composers, and about her appearances for various musical societies and on *The Lyrics Board* and the fun we had. I also interviewed Milo O'Shea, who was based in New York at the time. He did two wonderful programmes with me and shared some happy memories of my Aunt Joan and my uncle Pat O'Rourke.

I have had the pleasure of meeting thousands of people connected with the Association of Irish Musical Societies, and of attending hundreds of productions. I directed more than a few of them myself! AIMS represents over 130 musical

Louise Studley, a regular guest on Theatre Nights

societies throughout Ireland. It runs a Youth Summer School, Adjudication and Awards Scheme, an annual choral festival and local workshops, in addition to supporting the 14,000 people involved in producing musicals. It was a sad day all round when RTÉ pulled the plug on *Theatre Nights* in 2000. It helped to generate interest among listeners about current productions and it formed a showcase for exceptional talent.

Chapter 11

If They Could See Me Now

*T*he *Lyrics Board.* Who could have imagined that RTÉ television's own, home-grown musical quiz would become such a hit, drawing in over half a million Irish viewers each week, or that the format would eventually be sold to more than twenty countries worldwide, including Russia and South Africa?

The idea had very simple beginnings. My good friend John Keogh was at the piano entertaining people at a Christmas party for the children's radio show *Scratch Saturday.* As the night wore on, people started to sing a line from a song, and then challenged others to sing the next line. Andy Ruane, presenter of the show, and Philip Kampff, its director, realised the idea had potential to become a quiz show, and spent the next few months devising the format. It comprised two teams, each with a piano-playing captain and two guests. One team chose a number off 'the lyrics board' and a word was revealed; they would instantly have to come up a song containing that word, and then they could pick another number. If there was any hesitation, that team lost its turn. The team that identified the song won the round.

With John Keogh at the Powerscourt Centre, Dublin –
front page of The Irish Times, *8 December 1993, and featured*
in the RTÉ Guide *(Photo by Matt Kavanagh,* The Irish Times)

The quiz was first broadcast in 1992. John Keogh captained one team while I captained the other, and from the beginning the banter was mighty – it was like playing a parlour game in someone's house. The wonderful Aonghus McNally as presenter attempted to keep order, and over the years we had an eclectic bunch of guests, including Jerry Lee Lewis, Tony Ward, Honor Heffernan, Daniel O'Donnell, Anna Manahan, Dana, Veronica Dunne, Twink, Val Joyce and Tony Kenny. The show ran for five seasons and featured almost everyone who was anyone in the Irish music business, and we put on specials, like the St Patrick's Day show in 1993.

It was just a bit of fun, but what appears as spontaneous and relaxed to the viewer is often the result of days of hard work. Most of the guests joined in the spirit of the thing but every so often there would be one who took it too seriously

129

The Lyrics Board, *RTÉ, St Patrick's Day Special, 1993,
with Aonghus McNally and John Keogh (RTÉ Archives)*

or who was too inhibited to sing along, but for the most part it was hugely enjoyable. The show became so popular that *The Irish Times* published a photograph of John and myself on its front page in December 1993. We were entertaining at an event to promote the forthcoming RTÉ Christmas schedule.

In January 1995 I presented the first Veronica Dunne Singing Competition live on RTÉ 2 television. Coincidentally, it was on the same night of the week that *The Lyrics Board* was shown on RTÉ 1, so no matter which Irish station viewers tuned into, they got me. At an editorial board meeting the next day the director general was not well pleased. He said that although he knew Kevin Hough was a man of many talents, bilocation could not be one of them.

I was on another couple of quiz shows. Mike Murphy presented a Christmas special on his *Murphy's Micro Quiz,* with all the contestants dressed in pantomime costume. That was no problem for me as I took on my old role of Buttons. My team was Derek Davis as a character from *Aladdin* and the gorgeous Olivia Tracey as Cinderella. The other show was *Play the Game,* a charades-based quiz presented by Ronan Collins. This featured Derek Davis and Twink, who seemed to take the game very seriously, but Ronan was a good man to have at the helm because he could milk it for every little laugh. The worst title I ever had to mime was *The Attack of the Killer Tomatoes.* Needless to say, our team lost that round.

It looked as if my spell on Irish television had drawn to a close but, out of the blue, I was given a reprieve. Larry Masterson was the producer of *Open House,* the afternoon show on RTÉ One. He offered me a weekly slot playing and singing songs from the musicals. I said I would be delighted if I could bring along a female singer as well, and this was agreed. My friend Ellen McElroy and myself would rehearse for a few hours in the Radio Centre and then head over to join Marty Whelan and Mary Kennedy at Studio 1. *Open House* was a good show with high ratings but it was axed, amid much protest, in 2004.

While all the fame and recognition that comes from being on television was great fun, I was still producing musicals and shows in Dublin and around the country, adjudicating competitions and presenting events, as well as having a thoroughly good time working at RTÉ Radio 1, and revelling in all the opportunities that offered.

One of those opportunities was to make history in RTÉ by presenting the first live musical on Irish radio. It came about like this. In 1991 Ann Walsh, producer on *The Gay Byrne Hour*, suggested the idea of a musical, with a view to involving the whole country in the selection of the singers. The series producer was Alex White, who would later become a politician, and then Cabinet Minister for Communications, Energy and Natural Resources. Alex got in touch to sound me out as to which musical would go down well with the listeners, and to ask if I would be the producer. The answer to the second question was an emphatic yes! and, after a little thought, the answer to the first was *Oklahoma!* with all those well-loved songs. There was some discussion over whether the show should be recorded, but I felt very strongly that it should go out live. People perform better on live broadcasts – they give that little extra because there is no second chance.

When we put out the call inviting singers to take part, we were overwhelmed with the response. Ann Walsh and myself took to the roads during the freezing months of November and December 1990. We travelled with a full outside broadcast unit so that some of the auditions could be aired on the show. In all, we went to eight centres. Gay just had to mention the venue two days in advance and the cream of the amateur musical societies (and their mammies) turned up in their droves. Ita Flynn (from *Live at Three*) was our accompanist. We listened to more than 500 singers, and as one hopeful followed another, I am afraid I gained a reputation for shouting 'Next!' in an effort to keep the thing moving along. I remember Ann saying at one point that if she heard one more person sing 'Memories' by Andrew Lloyd Webber, she would scream. There were a few tears and even arguments over our selections from some of the contestants, but we were so impressed by the talent we discovered that we could have cast that show four times over. Eventually we whittled it down to ten principals and one hundred members for the chorus. Just one part was pre-cast, the small character role of Andrew Cairns, Ado Annie's father. After a great deal of coaxing from me, Gay agreed to do it, and he threw himself into it with gusto. There were two weekends of intensive rehearsals with musical director Jimmy Cavanagh before the show. Soloists and chorus travelled from all corners of the country and were hosted in nearby hotels, but mind you, they had to work hard.

Such was the level of publicity, I knew that reporters and photographers would be at the doors of Studio 1 on the morning of the performance, so I asked Wardrobe in RTÉ to supply costumes for the principals to add to the air of festivity. Two hours before the broadcast, over one hundred amateur singers nervously assembled for a final run-through with the RTÉ Concert Orchestra.

At nine o'clock on Monday, 14 January 1991 eager listeners tuned in from homes, shops, work, even schools to hear the first ever live performance of a musical on Irish radio. Everyone was on top form. The two leads, Jackie Winkless from Drogheda and Sandra Kelly from Dublin, were outstanding, Gay acquitted himself ably and the whole event was a resounding success. Madigan's of Donnybrook was the venue for the big end of show party and many of the people in the chorus had a chance to display their talents in a singsong that lasted for hours.

In 1993 Gay told me he was keen to present a concert at the National Concert Hall, and that the *Gay Byrne Show* had decided to produce another musical, *The Pirates of Penzance*.

The Pirates of Penzance, *Gay Byrne Show, RTÉ Radio 1, 1994*
(Photo by Maxwell Photography, RTÉ Archives)

So that winter I was on the road again to cast the leads and chorus of *Pirates*, to be aired on 21 March 1994. I always liked to have a chorus of about one hundred, not only for the big sound, but to give parts to as many good singers as possible. Auditions took place in venues that included Belfast, Derry and Donegal and were just as competitive as they had been in 1991, but I had difficulty finding a suitable tenor for the leading role of Frederic. I rang up Ronnie Dunne and she sent along a doctor whom, she said, was a fine singer. Once I heard his voice, I cast him straight away. That man was Ronan Tynan, who later became famous as one of the Irish Tenors. The Dublin auditions revealed two other singers who pursued successful careers, Miriam Murphy and Nyle Wolfe.

I was also selecting singers for *The Gay Byrne Show Gala Concert*, due to be staged before *Pirates*. The production of two distinct events with all the planning, decisions and organisation required for both kept me busy, to say the least.

The Gala Concert was broadcast live on *The Gay Byrne Show*. I was worried about asking singers to perform at the crack of dawn, but at 9 o'clock on the morning of 17 February 1994, the 25 soloists, one hundred chorus members, the RTÉ Concert Orchestra with conductor Jimmy Cavanagh, and a packed auditorium at the National Concert Hall were primed and ready for the show. Gay compèred the two-hour extravaganza of songs from the musicals, and joined in the rousing finale, 'The Black Hills of Dakota'. While he would readily admit that his voice is on the croaky side, Gay's enthusiasm is unsurpassed and infectious. Largely thanks to him, that concert and *The Pirates of Penzance*, broadcast live from Studio One in the Radio Centre on Monday 21 March 1994, drew in a huge listenership and attracted rave press reviews.

I had hardly drawn breath after all that excitement when Gay asked me to join him on a *Late Late Show* special to introduce some of our very talented radio singers to the tele-

Co-presenting The Late Late Show Special *with Gay, 1994*
(Photo by Maxwell Photography, RTÉ Archives)

vision public. Rehearsals for the show took place in the Radio Centre, and there was feverish excitement when the television people came over to time all the numbers and discuss camera shots and costumes. After the final rehearsal we were given vouchers to eat our fill at the RTÉ canteen, but some of the singers were too nervous to avail of this largesse, and were on tenterhooks waiting for the call for all the principals to go to Makeup and Wardrobe.

On Saturday 15 April 1994 I found it hard to believe that I was co-presenting the most popular show on Irish television with the legendary Gay Byrne. Our singers were all stars that night: Aisling Madden, Ray Barror, Paul Hennessy, Claudine Day, Ronan Tynan, Jackie Winkless, Anita Kerr, Siobhan Fawsitt and many more. Some members of the R&R chorus joined us, including Imelda Bradley and Joan La Grue. I am proud to say there were a few Hough girls there was well – Maura, Patricia, Phil and Fionnuala – and that my niece, Gráinne Gormley, conducted the orchestra. The chorus was so large, it occupied all the seats in Studio 1. I would have loved to have been in someone's sitting room for the surprise of seeing all those in attendance stand up and burst into song. Gay was, as always, kindness itself, and at the end of the evening when he announced there would be prizes for everyone in the audience, the cheers brought the house down. They each received a hamper and tickets for a sailing to England, and of course there was a huge party afterwards. What a night!

Chapter 12

The Midnight Special

If there's a show in town, then I want to see it, or be in it!
Muriel Quinn produced popular dinner/cabaret evenings in the Braemor Rooms in Churchtown, County Dublin,
and a Saturday night would often find me there with Larry
Gogan and his late wife Florrie, who was great pals with my
sister Fionnuala. Some of the acts moved between there and
the cabaret in Clontarf Castle. In the early 1990s Brendan
Grace had a regular act in the Braemor Rooms and he asked
me to do a slot on it. When Eileen Reid heard about that
she told me bluntly that my usual dinner jacket attire would
not do for this sort of gig at all. She took me along to her
friend James Fagan on Thomas Street who tailored clothes
for the showbands. Once there, she absolutely insisted on
buying me a sharp new three-piece suit in royal blue, which
I must admit looked the part. Choreographer Pat Conway
devised a tap routine for me and Billy Brown arranged all
my songs. Rose Tynan was on the bill and I shared a dressing
room with her. Apart from being an excellent singer, she was
a great woman with whom to share a joke. She was always
complaining about how difficult it was for her to lose weight,

but every night after the show she would get fish and chips to take home. On our opening night Gay Byrne and his wife Kathleen came to the show. The next morning Gay gave us a good plug on his radio programme and it had a lot to do with the success of the run.

Shannon's Restaurant in Stillorgan was an old stomping ground for me. I had a long-standing arrangement to play piano there six nights a week. Every other Sunday Mark Shannon and I would dine together. The tour manager for the 1993 production of *Cats*, which was on in the Point Depot on North Wall Quay, came for lunch. The show was finishing and he was planning an end-of-run party. He asked me if I would play at it and I agreed, assuming it would be backstage or at some nearby restaurant. He promised to send a taxi because it would be a late night do. I was duly collected, and shortly before midnight, with not a sound from the pavement, we arrived at Heuston Station. It seemed an odd venue for a party, but I was told there was a train waiting. Not only that, but they had removed a window from the train to hoist a piano inside. Intrigued, I climbed on board to find the cast and directors and people who worked in the Point, including cleaners, front of house and management, all rearing to go, and go we did.

The train powered up and, as we sped through the Irish countryside, there was no end to the fun. I played in one carriage and a trio entertained in another. Platefuls of food kept coming and when someone asked for a glass of champagne they were given a bottle. The cast were the kindest of people and everyone joined in to sing all the old songs. At about six in the morning we pulled back into Dublin and piled out of the train, somewhat the worse for wear but very happy. It has to go down as the most remarkable after-show party I ever had the good fortune to attend.

Maureen O'Hara came to Shannon's one night and she joined me at the piano. I played all her favourites, including 'The Kerry Cow' and some John Wayne movie themes. I owned a book entitled *Close Up* about the legends of stage and screen that I asked all the stars I worked with to autograph. When Maureen signed her page, she asked if she might have a photocopy of it. I was delighted to arrange that, and the next morning she called into RTÉ on her way to the airport to fly back to the States. I gave her the copy and had some pictures taken with her. Hollywood directors said that her profile was so perfect, you got a wonderful shot whatever angle it was taken from, and all I can say is that her personality matched her profile.

With Maureen O'Hara at RTÉ, Donnybrook, 1993

I was occasionally asked to play the piano at events in the American Ambassador's Residence in the Phoenix Park. When Jean Kennedy Smith was appointed Ambassador in 1993 I became a regular there, the arrangement being that I would bring along a male vocalist and perform Irish songs for the guests. Notice was always short, so I would have to jump when I got the call and I often ended up at home rehearsing with the singer just before the gig. The piano in the residence was a Kimball, which I imagine had been shipped from the manufacturers in Chicago. It was a beautiful instrument and a great pleasure to play because they kept it in tip-top condition. A photograph of Jean and her brother JFK was on permanent display on the piano. Each time I lifted it off to open the lid, it always struck me how alike they both were.

I never knew the names of the guests until after I had arrived, and then I would try to tailor the numbers to please them, but sometimes I got it wrong. The gorgeous Lauren Bacall was there one night, so I played a selection of tunes from Humphrey Bogart films. I knew they had been madly in love and that Lauren nursed him through his last illness, but that had been nearly 40 years before. As I was playing I realised, all too late, that she was sitting stony-faced in the corner. Perhaps she was weary of perpetually being linked with Bogie and not celebrated for everything she had done since, but she was good enough to sign my book. When Carly Simon was a guest, I got a break, because she just sat down at the piano as relaxed as anything and played and sang her own melodious songs.

Another regular was John Hume. His party piece was 'The Town I Loved so Well'. One night as I was getting ready to play for the after dinner drinks, John wandered out of the dining room to have a smoke and we chatted. I asked if he was going to sing the usual and he said, 'Yes. Will you just give me the note, so I'll be sure to start off in the right key?'

I hit the note and a waiter came flying out of the dining room saying, 'The Ambassador said you are not to play until she tells you.' I explained that I was only checking the key for John Hume but the waiter said, 'It doesn't matter. Do not play until you are told to.'

Jean Kennedy Smith was a tough lady but I got on really well with her. Mind you, I always had to enter through the servants' entrance, even though I was in black tie. Security was tight. Each time I drove in, I had to be checked through the gate, the car bonnet was lifted and the boot examined, but I loved playing there and would gladly do so again. My good pal Noel O'Shea, the tree surgeon in the Phoenix Park, says he will put in a word for me!

I was invited to the American Embassy in Ballsbridge for a function at which soldiers were receiving awards. I provided background music before and during the meal. For no particular reason I started to play 'Tammy', the Debbie Reynolds song in *Tammy and the Bachelor*. A big guy, probably one of the soldiers, came over and began to sing it in a deep velvety voice. We got talking, and he told me the song was one of his favourites. That prompted me to ask if he would sing a favourite of mine, 'Ol' Man River', which I knew would display his magnificent bass voice. He said he would be delighted, so I stood up from the piano and did my 'Hello, good evening and welcome' bit and introduced him. As he sang, there was a breathless stillness in the room. When he finished, the place erupted into prolonged applause. I do not know who he was, but that night that man was a star. I returned home on a high and I am sure he did too.

While I love to play piano, I get a great kick out of presenting and narrating as well, and have been fortunate that Cathal MacCabe has given me the opportunity to do both. Cathal and I have been involved in many productions together. Our friendship goes back to 1968 when he made the move from Derry to Dublin to work as a producer in RTÉ Radio. He became controller of 2FM in 1986, and in 1992 was appointed Head of Music in RTÉ. Cathal is an extraordinarily talented guy. In addition to all his responsibilities with RTÉ, he has sung lead roles in several shows, directed world premieres of Irish musicals and productions for societies up and down the country – he was the director when I was in *Irene* and *Bottler in Nipperland* – and he is a French speaker. Ever ready to consider new projects, Cathal has often helped me out by writing scripts or amending musicals to suit different groups.

I presented and recorded concerts for a variety of radio programmes. In 2002 Cathal approached me in connection with a series of thirteen concerts celebrating the music of the musicals. Each show was scripted and directed by him, and I had the great pleasure of introducing the music that I love from the stage of the National Concert Hall. We did tributes to Doris Day, Mario Lanza, Maurice Chevalier, Gordon MacRae, Jeanette MacDonald, Nelson Eddy, The MGM Musicals, A Victorian Christmas, George Gershwin, Cole Porter, Sigmund Romberg, Ivor Novello and Noël Coward. Because the concerts were to be broadcast on RTÉ later in the year, they were all promoted on radio, which boosted ticket sales, and we got great crowds. It was a wonderful experience.

One of Cathal's recent ventures was *I Hear You Calling Me: The Story of Count John McCormack* in 2011. Cathal devised and directed the show that celebrates the life and music of Ireland's most famous tenor. He chose some of McCormack's best-loved songs, 'Roses of Picardy', 'Macushla', 'I Dreamt That I Dwelt In Marble Halls', 'Because', 'I Hear You Calling Me' and many more, to illuminate the story that I narrated. The

I Hear You Calling Me: The Story of Count John McCormack, *2011*

brilliant Michael Casey was our musical director and pianist, and with Waterford tenor Frank Ryan in the title role, Cork soprano Linda Kenny as Lily and violinists Daniel and Tim Lehane, we quickly realised we had a hit on our hands. Audiences loved the combination of the story and those marvellous old songs that they could hum-along to. The show was so popular that we toured the country for nearly two years without a break.

But Cathal did not rest on the laurels of John McCormack. During the run he was busy working on his next show, *Blaze Away! The Incredible Story of Josef Locke*, which opened in 2013. Cathal was born just 300 yards from the butcher's shop in Derry owned by the father of Joseph McLaughlin (Locke's birth name), and he met Locke on several occasions. The darling of the London stage in the 1940s and 1950s, Josef

Locke led a scandalous life of womanising, heartbreak and tax-dodging. This provided Cathal with plenty of lively material, interspersed with old favourites, including 'Hear My Song, Violetta', 'I'll Walk Beside You', 'The Old Bog Road' and, of course, 'Blaze Away': '*... as the bonfire keeps on burning, happy days will be returning, while the band keeps playing we'll let our troubles blaze away.*'

There was a cast of four, and the idea was that I would narrate the story and the others would enact it. The show began and I launched into telling the scandal of a senior government minister, an attractive dark-haired lady and our hero Josef. I was interrupted by the appearance of a big fellow purporting to be the 'real' Josef Locke who said it was all a pack of lies, and anyway the lady was not dark, she was a redhead! The scene was set for a riotous evening of spirited banter between the players, and Joe O'Gorman, Frank Ryan, Linda Kenny and myself enjoyed it every bit as much as our audiences. With Michael Casey as musical director the show was a huge success.

I was back to singing again in 2014 for *The Very Best of Broadway*, presented by Mill Productions in Dundrum, County Dublin. Garry Mountaine and myself made the most of 'Brush Up Your Shakespeare', 'Kiss Me Kate', 'Annie Get Your Gun' and 'Anything You Can Do', and in all modesty I can say that I have done just about everything I wanted to do in theatre, bar playing Hamlet or flying the high trapeze, and had the best of times doing it.

Chapter 13

Let's Go On With the Show

There really is no business like it.

As a director, I get everything thrown at me – auditions, arguments over cast selection, poorly equipped halls, terrible costumes, scenery, props, lighting and sound, fraught rehearsals with 'it'll be alright on the night' merchants, temperamental musical directors, soloists with sore throats, dancers who think an exercise barre is lifting a pint in a pub, and front-of-house who like nothing more than a chinwag when confronted with a queue of potential attendees. And sometimes it goes swimmingly.

When I first started out directing musicals, I thought I had a fair grasp of what was involved. I had played in so many and managed one; I had kept my eyes and ears open, helped out whenever I could. But of course I had so much to learn that can only be learned on the job – being the guy everyone turns to for guidance, being the guy who has the plan for the whole show in his head, and who has to be able to communicate it and enthuse people, and even about being the fall guy when everything goes hopelessly wrong.

In the early 1970s my first venture into directing had gone well, and in 1976 the Greystones Operatic and Dramatic Society asked me to direct *The Boy Friend* by Sandy Wilson. Greystones was a go-ahead society with musical director Peggy O'Neill, and a cohort of good singers that they would augment when necessary with members of the R&R. Over the years I ended up doing thirteen productions for them, including *The Pirates of Penzance, Magyar Melody, No No Nanette* and *The Merry Widow,* many of which featured their leading light, the talented Barbara Graham. David Fitzgerald, owner of the La Touche Hotel in Greystones, was a fervent Gilbert & Sullivan fan and a dedicated supporter of the society. When we were in town to do a show, David threw open the hospitality of the hotel to myself and members of the R&R, and we all had a thoroughly good time.

That same year I directed *Waltzes from Vienna* for the Bray Musical Society. It was their entry for the 1976 Waterford International Festival of Music. We ran it for a week in Bray and then took it to Waterford to compete. The society had talented players and experienced leads in Colette Donnelly, Frank Cullinane and Ruth Dodd. The adjudicator commented that it was a very artistic production, the show scooped five awards, and I was cock-a-hoop.

After that, my career really took off. In 1977 the Glasnevin Musical Society asked me to direct a major production of Johann Strauss's *The Gypsy Baron* at the Gaiety Theatre. This was doubly exciting – my first experience directing in the Gaiety, and my first time directing my sister Fionnuala, who was playing the lead soprano role, Arsena. While in some respects it was hard work, in others it was fantastic because we had a great cast, including Ramon Remedios who was an excellent Barinkay. It is a measure of Fionnuala's talent that, following the show, she was engaged by English National Opera North. She toured all over England with them, and two years later was invited to join them for a major production in Venice. That *Gypsy Baron* opened up a whole new career for me, too. After the rave reviews it received in the press, musical societies began to seek me out and I have been going up and down the country directing musicals ever since.

My first engagement outside Dublin was in the late 1970s with the Tullamore Musical Society for a production of *Magyar Melody*, subtitled *A Romance with Music*. I had seen it years before in St. Louis' Convent, Rathmines when Fionnuala played the male lead. I loved the music, but the story was so out of date. I always remember the last line from one of the main characters, Michael, who is a composer. He tells his leading lady that he will write a musical for her and will call it *Happy Ever After.* These days a title like that would raise a wry laugh.

Some societies tend to be very professional, while others want to put on a good show *and* have a jolly good time. The Tullamore people were enthusiastic, and a special stage was erected in the function room of the Bridge House Hotel where a large attendance was guaranteed. I had asked the performers to comport themselves like professionals by changing backstage and not allowing the audience to see them in character before the show. What happened on the first night? As I was walking to the venue, I saw a member of the chorus, who incidentally was also the chorus mistress, parading down the main street in Tyrolean costume – headdress, ribbons flying and in full theatrical makeup. I could swear I heard her declare, 'I am in the opera'.

The show was going well until I noticed that trays of beer were being delivered backstage. By the third act, the male singers were well lubricated, and cues started to go out the window. As soon as the curtain came down I called the chairman, who explained that if I banned the pints, not only would they not get the venue the next year, but they would have no society. I was only around for the opening night so I had no choice but to leave them to it, but I could never approve of drinking during a show when you need all your wits about you. I had the same problem in Gorey, County Wexford. I agreed to direct *Annie Get Your Gun* with them, and Cathal MacCabe and I went to see their production of *South Pacific* beforehand. During the interval we saw Bloody Mary and a bunch of the sailors swilling pints in the pub across the road. We couldn't believe it. But there was worse to come. During the second half when some of the chorus and cast were not on stage, they came out front to have a look at the show. That sort of thing was unheard of in any company I had worked with.

The musical society in Clontarf was excellent. I directed two shows for them – *La Vie Parisienne* and *The Sorcerer*. When I arrived for the first rehearsal, they were word perfect on each occasion and knew every note of the score. They also had a very talented hairdresser from Fairview who had worked with me previously when I played Madam Lucy, the dress designer in the O'Connell Musical Society production of *Irene*. I was telling friends how musically good the Clontarf society was and they said, 'Of course they're good. Don't they sing in church every Sunday morning?' Later I realised just how good church singers are when I produced the Mass and Services for RTÉ Radio 1. The congregations in the Church of

Ireland, Presbyterian and Methodist services were the best. I am sorry to say that when I produced Catholic services, I had to beg them to sing out.

In Dublin, I directed the Fitzpatrick's Irish Cabaret in The Dungeon at Killiney Castle, County Dublin – a dinner and cabaret show beloved by American tourists. There was Irish dancing, fiddle playing by Kevin Glackin, singing with baritone Philip Byrne and comedy with Danny Cummins. My sister Patricia performed, and Marie-Louise O'Donnell sang and played her guitar, and also had duets with her sister, a brilliant harpist. Marie-Louise is now a most engaging contributor on RTÉ Radio 1, and is an outspoken member of Seanad Éireann. Her mother Maura Cranny taught most of us Hough children elocution in St Louis' School in Rathmines, and that is why we all talk so proper! Danny was nearing the end of his career but he was still a very funny man. I remember seeing him in *Gales of Laughter*, that perennial summer variety show in the Gaiety. He and Maureen Potter had a hilarious routine as ballroom dancers. Maureen wore a dress with ten thousand sequins, designed and made by Babs De Monte, and Danny had a dreadful stick-on moustache.

In 1985 I was asked to direct a concert of Irish poetry, music and dance for The Brendan Society at the National Concert Hall. I was keen for Siobhan McKenna to make a guest appearance. Renowned for her beauty and her voice with its soft, West of Ireland accent that conveyed so much meaning, I knew no one could carry a poem like Siobhan. She had just finished a show in the Gaiety in which she and Maureen Potter played the two old ladies in *Arsenic and Old Lace* with great verve.

Siobhan McKenna and Maureen Potter
in Arsenic and Old Lace, *1985*

Despite being unwell, Siobhan's agent told me that since Gay Byrne was presenting the show, she would like to perform. It was a lovely evening. We had the Festive Ensemble, baritone Frank O'Brien, the Pat Conway Dancers, soprano Kathryn Smith, Ita Flynn on piano and The Rory O'Connor Irish Dancers. We also had harpists and a beautiful set designed by Fiona Morris. Siobhan recited beautifully, as I knew she would. The one downside to the event was that the producers asked why I had paid so much for her appearance. I replied because she is probably the most successful Irish actress ever to work in film and theatre both at home and abroad. It was a desperate loss when Siobhan died of lung cancer the following year, aged only sixty-three.

I had been nineteen in 1963 when I attended a ball at the Shelbourne Hotel, Dublin to commemorate the fiftieth anniversary of the legendary Rathmines and Rathgar Musical Society. Did I ever imagine that thirty years later that same society would ask me to direct a significant show for them on a historic occasion? Gilbert & Sullivan's *The Mikado* was the musical that launched the R&R in the old Queen's Theatre on Pearse Street, Dublin in 1913, and they wished to celebrate eighty glorious years with a new production and with me at the helm. I was deeply honoured. As rehearsals got under way with the keen and accomplished cast, I had a feeling that, out of all the *Mikado*s I had directed in the past, this was going to be the best.

The show was presented in the National Concert Hall and ran for nine nights in October 1993. It was a staged production with ingenious sets by Patrick Murray, a full orchestra led by Gearóid Grant, and chorus and dancers. Alison Roddy and Paul Kelly sparkled as the lovers Yum-Yum and Nanki-Poo. Miriam Murphy's powerful voice added dramatic intensity as Katisha, Emer Hartnett was a vivacious Pitti-Sing, Ray Barror's Ko-Ko and Adam Lawlor's Pooh-Bah played off each other beautifully. Robert McKevitt as the Mikado nearly stole the show during his brief second act appearance. I was

The Mikado *at the National Concert Hall. R&R Musical Society, 1993*

151

so happy for everyone, especially the R&R, when the production was a big hit with audiences and lavished with praise in the press. In *The Irish Times,* Ian Fox commented that *The Mikado* was played with 'such panache and vivacity' that it was 'the highlight of the current festival activities. Gilbert & Sullivan's frolic is given a bubbling production by Kevin Hough, well balanced between tradition and innovation.'

It was a time for anniversaries. In 1994, the Cecilian Musical Society in Limerick wanted to put on *The Merry Widow* to celebrate their seventy-five years. Costumes were specially ordered from England, but when our beautiful soprano Joan Merrigan appeared on stage at the dress rehearsal, I took one look at her outfit and knew it would not do at all – it was for a member of chorus and not for a leading lady. I complained to the chairman of the committee, but because the show was opening the next night he was at a loss as to what to do. I phoned all the costumiers in Dublin. My old reliable Burke's had closed and no one had anything suitable at such short notice. I was really in trouble, but the society did have a seamstress, and we rushed out and bought yards of lilac material. That lady worked miracles, and on opening night Joan appeared in the most beautiful dress I have ever seen for the widow. Alas, the drama did not end there. The baritone Philip Byrne, who was a great friend and a lovely guy to work with, played Danilo. He stepped on Joan's train in the famous waltz scene and *rrrippp* – we feared the dress was ruined. However, our wonderful seamstress got to work and had it perfect for the next performance.

Joan and I have worked a few times together. Some months after that show, we took part in an evening at the National Concert Hall devoted to the music of Ivor Novello.

Proinnsías Ó Duinn, Joan's partner, conducted the RTÉ Concert Orchestra. I loved working with Proinnsías – he always got the balance right and was so encouraging. Singers need support and he gave it one hundredfold. I sang some comedy numbers like 'Bees Are Buzzin'' and 'Her Mother Came Too', we had a fine tenor from Wales, and Joan was in top form with songs that really suited her voice. When I listened back to the recording before it was broadcast on *Theatre Nights*, I regretted that we never toured with that show – it was one of the best gigs I have ever done.

A director friend of mine got a call from a society to ask if he would direct *Ipi Tombi* for them and could he quote a fee. *Ipi Tombi* is a pulsating dance and music celebration of black South African culture. Exciting to stage, but tricky. Where are you going to find bare-breasted, loose-hipped women, fearless half-naked fellows, a battery of drummers and a clutch of Zulu dancers in the midlands of Ireland? My friend asked the society's chairman if he had seen the show and he said ah no, they just thought they would do something that no one else in the region had done and also the name would look good on a poster. When it was explained to him about the costumes, or the lack thereof, he changed his mind, and suggested *The Merry Widow*. With that, my friend threw his hat at it and passed the buck on to me.

When the society approached me, I asked for a video of their previous year's production of *The King and I* to give me some idea of their strengths. My heart sank as the opening scene rolled. Anna was about to board the boat to meet the King of Siam when Captain Orton uttered the deathless phrase, 'Okay then, I will see you tomorrow night in the Hazel Hotel for a pint.' The very idea of Mrs Anna knocking back a pint does not bear thinking about. I could only surmise that the hotel had taken an advert in the programme and therefore demanded a plug from the stage. However, I like to give everyone a chance, so I went down and conducted three audition sessions. The guy who was to play Danilo was much too old for the part, and no one at all turned up to audition for the role of Anna or the second lead, Valencienne. It was no good; I could not work with them. They offered to pay my expenses and of course I said I would not hear of it and drove home much relieved.

In Athlone, a leading lady had a dental plate and at the end of the first act one centre tooth flew off during an aria. All during the second act she held her hand in front of her mouth as she sang her love duets. Near the end of the show, a dentist was found in the town and I believe a tube of super glue was flourished and the tooth was stuck back in time for the final curtain call.

The business of casting can be a minefield when it comes to some societies who, year after year, give the best parts to the same people. I was directing *Oklahoma!* in County Galway and I decided to cast new singers to give them experience and perhaps liven up the show. It did not go down well with the committee but I stuck to my guns. Then it came to choosing who would play Ado Annie. The lady auditioning had once been a Bunratty singer and she was married to the local bank manager, who also happened to be the chairman of the society, but she was all wrong for the role of the flirty young girl. When I said I would like someone else to try for it, I was promptly called to a meeting. After a futile discussion, I gave in and accepted her, partly because I thought that if they lost money on the show, they would need the husband to bail them out.

The lady in question did not want to appear foolish on stage by playing Ado Annie as a stupid girl. I tried to remain patient as I explained the humour in Ado Annie asking her dad 'Hey Pa, what you been shootin'?' and he standing there in front of her with a fistful of rabbits. There were a couple of redeeming features to the whole escapade. The two young leads were strong and I am sure they appeared in many subsequent productions, and the landlady in my digs near Salthill was an excellent cook, and it is not every day you can say that.

I directed *Oklahoma!* again for the Briery Gap Theatre in Macroom, County Cork in 2010. This marked their tenth anniversary of a successful initiative to bring a varied programme of entertainment to the busy market town of Macroom and the entire Lee Valley. They produced a panto the year before I was to direct, so I went along to see what the talent was like and spotted two people who would be perfect in *Oklahoma!* They later auditioned and were excellent.

I travelled by train to Cork and stayed for rehearsals in Macroom. There was a great feeling about the theatre, lots of energy and enthusiasm, but the space was limited. During the dress rehearsal Ado Annie said she did not have enough room to come on side stage with the chorus in position. I reminded her that we were not playing the Gaiety but the Briery Gap. 'Darling,' I said, 'push the chorus members out of your way – that's what a principal does!'

Getting realistic props is always a problem. I asked the fellow who was playing Cairns if he could find something that looked like real rabbits for his first entrance. He did better than that. He went out to the local golf course and shot a few! I could not believe it when I saw him at the first dress rehearsal with the rabbits tied and thrown over his shoulder. The smell in the dressing room must have been awful after the first few performances but it just goes to prove how committed the members of some societies are to putting on a good show. When I directed *Showboat* with them, someone was sent to a local farmer to collect bales of hay. They arrived in good time, but amongst the hay was a decomposing fox and some dead rats!

In 2012 we staged a sparkling production of *Calamity Jane*, with Stephanie Shine as Calamity and Pat Mullane as Wild Bill Hickock. The following year the theatre underwent a major refurbishment, but I was with them again in 2014 for a production of *The Sound of Music*. Although I was very unwell during rehearsals, I soldiered on with the help of antibiotics and painkillers and, thankfully, the show carried the day. All seven performances were a sell-out, and after each there were standing ovations and cheers for the principals and the talented young cast. It was so popular that the Everyman Palace Theatre requested a special performance in Cork city, so in June we transferred sets, costumes, props and some very excited entertainers to that splendid venue, and the show went down a storm. My last production with the company was *Oliver!* in 2015. That show also went to the Everyman where we packed them in.

I am not sure that the musical society scene is as thriving as it once was. Emigration not only decimated local communities and sports teams, it also affected musical societies. The culture of Xbox and *X Factor* are having an effect too. A lot of young people seem to be more interested in being entertained than in entertaining themselves, and those who do seek fame and fortune try to achieve it instantly by being a solo performer or part of a band or winning a talent competition. If they only realised the fun and laughs to be had when participating in a show and all the great musical training they would receive – it certainly was a super proving ground for me, and for many of the people I have met on my travels. There is something for everyone. Singing and acting, stagecraft, lighting and sound, costumes, design and painting, producing and directing, writing, makeup, front of house, publicity, arranging venues, accommodation and transport, working with people, learning tolerance and leadership. These are crafts and skills that, once experienced and acquired, enrich life and encourage an appreciation of one of the oldest forms of culture – theatre. Irving Berlin got it just right when he said there is no business like show business. I would not change it for a sack of gold, although gold would be nice too!

Chapter 14

I've Got a Little List

You might not think that working in a shop on the Crumlin Road was a great preparation for life in the theatre, but dealing with all kinds of people gave me confidence, and I acquired basic organisational skills that I was able to build on when producing or managing musicals. Any time you see a stage show, a play, a musical or a revue, you have to remember that a great deal of time and planning occurs before opening night. The venue and the artists have to be booked. Music has to be arranged and a band or orchestra engaged. Costumes may have to be hired, and if the show is to go on tour, accommodation has to be organised. You could say it was like keeping the shop supplied with fresh produce, and making sure the staff and customers were happy.

From my first tentative steps in the 1970s, I have produced more shows that I can count. Many have been talent competitions, either as a show on their own, or as auditions for a performance. For a number of years I produced the Tipperary Song Contest. One year Joe Lynch was the MC, and I prepared a couple of pages giving him details of the contestants and wrote the script for all his links. Joe missed the rehearsals so I filled in for him at the run-through. When he arrived for the show he was wearing brown shoes with his black dress suit. Now, this is just the sort of detail that drives me mad because the audience and the cameras always pick up on it. He was a size eight and I am a size eight so we switched shoes. In the middle of the show Joe announced that song eight was the last song of the evening (it must have had something to do with the shoes), but there were four more songs to come. The audience started muttering and I had to shout at him from the wings. He apologised and the performances resumed.

The year that Gay Byrne was the MC, Ruth Buchanan and Lynn Geldof were amongst the adjudicators. Lynn was an absolute hoot and great company. One of the contestants was a really stuck-up guy from England. He had an excellent voice and I was sure he was going to win, but for some reason or other he got up Lynn's nose, so when it came to marking him she gave him only ten points out of a possible fifty. All the other adjudicators gave him high marks but that was not enough for him to win. He demanded to see the adjudicators' comments and I had to tell him that it was not in our brief to reveal the comments. He was understandably furious and complained to Gay that the whole thing had been a fix.

That evening Gay was enjoying a well-earned drink in the hotel when a lady whose husband was a Church of Ireland minister cornered him. The husband was fundraising for a new roof for his church or some such thing and she thought he would make an excellent guest on *The Late Late Show*. I noticed that she obviously was not going to take no for an answer, so I quietly drew Gay aside and asked if he wanted to be rescued. He was grateful for the thought but declined. He is as courteous off air as he is on air, and in the end he managed to escape the lady's clutches. Such are the joys of fame.

Ann Darcy of the Clontarf Castle Hotel asked me to organise not one but four talent competitions for them, to be run over a four-week period. There were to be no judges. Instead, the audience would vote for their favourites. As you can imagine, this was a great crowd-puller with each contestant roping in as many supporters as possible. One night, busloads came from Ballyfermot, and the winner was not a singer but a ballet dancer.

I have been in some wonderful parts of the country in my quest for talent, but few can equal the scenery that lies between Rathdrum and Arklow in County Wicklow. In 1807 the poet Thomas Moore caught the serenity of the place in his poem 'The Meeting of the Waters':

> *Sweet vale of Avoca! how calm could I rest*
> *In thy bosom of shade, with the friends I love best,*
> *Where the storms that we feel in this*
> *   cold world should cease,*
> *And our hearts, like thy waters, be mingled in peace.*

Avoca was the setting for the Guinness Melody Fair, a weeklong festival dedicated to Thomas Moore, and in 1997 I was appointed producer and presenter of The Moore Singer of the Year competition. With a top prize of £1,000, the competition was an important event, and I selected Cathal MacCabe, Jane Carty, the renowned music jury member, and Proinnsías Ó Duinn, principal conductor of the RTÉ Concert Orchestra, as adjudicators. I was glad I recorded the finals for *Theatre Nights* because the competition attracted many Feis Ceol winners and the standard was exceptional. The same could not be said about the standard of the piano at the venue, the Vale View Hotel, but we had it patched up and tuned, and it met our needs over the next three years. The festival got off to an explosive start in the millennium year of 2000 with a spectacular display of fireworks, which appealed not only to Moore devotees but also to fans of the sitcom *Ballykissangel*, filmed on location at Avoca – 'the town where everybody knows each other's business'. Sadly, that was the last year I was involved because the hotel was extensively damaged by fire in 2001. The damage also put paid to a countrywide children's singing contest that I ran alongside the Singer of the Year.

In my trips around the country I have often remarked that Ireland is coming down with talent, but I thought that the older generation were not getting a look in. The Dublin Docklands Development Authority got in touch with me in 2003 in connection with their social regeneration projects. There has been an incredible amount of building and investment in the east of Dublin along both banks of the River Liffey. While the infrastructure and shiny new offices were growing apace, the Authority was concerned that the old neighbourhoods might lose their cohesion, and a host of community schemes were encouraged and sponsored. That is where I came in. I suggested an over-60s competition, and the Docklands Senior Citizens Talent Showcase was inaugurated.

We auditioned more than fifty acts and selected twelve for the grand finale at the Abbey Theatre, including a singing duo in their seventies, an 81-year-old violinist and a 94-year-old singer. It was a wonderfully happy event, and the six experienced adjudicators, led by Maureen Potter and Val Joyce, had a hard task choosing the winner. Sean Caulfield from Ringsend eventually walked away with €750 and an engraved piece of Dublin Crystal for his superb rendition of 'Bring Him Home'. The Showcase proved so popular that I produced it for the next five years, alongside a children's talent showcase that I produced and presented in the National Concert Hall, which was every bit as joyous and successful.

When the Docklands Authority asked me to run a series of theatre classes for the children in the area, I was delighted to do it. I wanted to offer hands-on experience of lots of different aspects of entertainment, so I booked Terenure College and gathered together a group of gifted friends to provide the training. Maggie Joyce had the spacious concert hall of the college in which to teach her dance classes with Dex McLoughlin and Catherine Casey, and Shelagh Cullen conducted make-up sessions in the classrooms. Michael Grennell, John Conroy and Kate Minogue supervised the drama. Don Conroy, the artist and television presenter, demonstrated and taught art. Jackie Curran and Ronan Johnson were in charge of lively music sessions. We ran it for four years every October during the mid-term break. The children were brought to Terenure by bus every day and were usually supervised by their own teachers. One day, however, I had to hire in outside supervisors. Some of the children saw this as an opportunity to become rowdy, and when they arrived at the college I had problems getting them to behave. It takes just a few to make trouble for everyone. It was very disheartening, but all you can do is sow the seeds and hope that some take root. Several of those children did go on to perform in later years, and one sang the lead in a musical at the Bord Gáis Theatre.

On the strength of the over-60s showcase success, I believed that RTÉ Radio could do something similar, but on a countrywide basis. The idea was discussed and welcomed, and the All Ireland Active Age Talent Showcase received official approval. From October 2004 to February 2005, musical director Andy O'Callaghan and I travelled to all thirty-two counties in search of the new Maureen Potter or Daniel O'Donnell. It was a huge undertaking, but our super co-ordinator Geralyn Aspill, took command of all arrangements and everything went smoothly. In each county we were faced with the task of auditioning and then selecting just one act to represent that county. This could be a soloist or a group, singing, playing an instrument, acting or providing some sort of entertainment that we hadn't even considered.

I did say that Ireland was coming down with talent, but it is also coming down with people who think they have talent so we sat through a few excruciating performances, but we also had some great laughs. One lady came on to perform a Marlene Dietrich number in what was supposed to be a smoky German cabaret voice. She said her children had pleaded with her not to do it. She was dressed in an extraordinary outfit with a see-through black nylon top and she was about as smoky as a packet of candy cigarettes. When she was finished, she announced, 'I am glad I did that. Now I am off to the dogs,' and indeed she was. In one of the Northern counties a man brought his own public address system and took about fifteen minutes to set it all up. I thought to myself that this guy looks good, but then he made the mistake of opening his mouth to sing a horrendous Country and Western number entitled 'Don't close the lid on the coffin until I kiss me mother goodbye', and I thought Andy was going to choke from holding in his laughter.

But those were the exceptions. When we arrived at the National Concert Hall at the end of March 2005 for the two days of finals, we had our thirty-two acts of outstanding amateur talent. Andy worked hard with the contestants in rehearsals and makeup artist Shelagh Cullen ensured that they looked marvellous. Veronica Dunne and Austin Gaffney headed the adjudicating panel, and Gay Byrne did a terrific job of hosting the event. The winner was Michael Blair from Belfast, who sang 'Every Day is Ladies Day for Me'. He was so good, he could easily have made it on the professional stage.

I knew the show had gone down well, but I was thrilled a couple of weeks later to receive this letter from Adrian Moynes, Managing Direction of RTÉ Radio.

Dear Kevin,

It's important to put on paper my regard for your achievement in conceiving and producing the Active Age Talent Contest. Everyone had two big nights at the NCH, and the performances were rewarded by the extraordinary atmosphere. Afterwards, so many audience members told me of their pleasure and of their appreciation of such good entertainment. I want to pass that on to you, and to thank you for carrying the flag in every county for so many months. All that hard work had a triumphant result.

I don't know what it is about travel and me – I just cannot keep off the roads of Ireland! In 2006 Lorelei Harris, RTÉ's editor of feature arts and documentaries, had a bright idea for a one-off production. We would again hold auditions all over the country, but this time would not reveal what show we were auditioning for – it was to be a 'Mystery Musical'. So Andy, my broadcasting assistant Geralyn and the crew and I hit the highways and byways. Occasionally we stopped at provincial RTÉ studios to do live broadcasts of the contestants for the Ronan Collins Afternoon Show. That publicity really spiked interest among the listeners and kept them guessing about the production and where it would be presented. In the spring of 2006 Ronan made the grand announcement that the mystery musical was to be *Carousel,* and it would be performed at the Helix Theatre, Dublin. We chose *Carousel* because it has one of the most beautiful scores in the Rogers and Hammerstein repertoire, and I knew it would suit the singers we had auditioned. But the contestants did not know they had been successful until we unveiled the cast list. That caused more excitement, and then we had to organise rehearsals for the principals and one hundred members of the chorus.

On Sunday, 28 May 2006 we all assembled in the Helix Theatre for the performance and recording of *Carousel,* with the RTÉ Concert Orchestra conducted by Gearóid Grant. The principals, including Sinead Gillespie from Donegal, Aoife O'Sullivan from Meath, Martin Hall from Dublin, and Margaret Keys from Derry (playing the role of Carrie, made famous by our own Jean Darling) took to the stage with the chorus and sang their hearts out. It was fabulous, and it was fitting to go out on such a great occasion – that was the last big show I did with the radio station.

On Thursday, 22 January 2009 I retired from RTÉ. They threw a party for me in Studio 1, and it was like the best after-show party I have even been at. I could not believe how many

*A gallant band of Broadcast Assistants at the retirement
party (front from left: Helen Howard, Jane Reid,
Noreen Nichol, Kevin, Siobhan Hough, Pauline O'Donnell,
Jo Wheatley, Joan Torsney; back from left: Deirdre Magee,
Geralyn Aspill, Lucia Proctor, Claire Byrne, Deirdre Ryan)
(Photo by Charles Byrne)*

friends turned up to wish me farewell, even Aunty Poppy.
Ronan Collins was the host and he sang a parody of 'Piano
Man', especially written by Ruth Buchanan. It was wonderful to see so many of my ex-broadcasting assistants gathered
together for once, probably telling each other salacious stories about me! My brother and all my sisters were there, and
they performed while I played piano. Ellen McElroy brought
along her three-piece band and they did their Andrews Sisters act. Twink unveiled her new talent by presenting me
with a stunning cake, which she had baked and decorated
herself. It featured a dial radio, theatre masks, a top hat and
cane and a pair of tap shoes on a stage. It was taken away
for photographs and I never saw it again, so if someone out
there has my retirement cake, please may I have it back? On

Twink with her high fidelity wireless cake
(Photo by Charles Byrne)

the other hand, it was such a work of art it would have been a shame to put a knife in it and actually take a bite.

Adrian Moynes presented me with a very nice painting and that should have been that, but it was not. Just before I retired I was on *The Ryan Tubridy Show* and I sang a song composed for me by Billy Brown:

I'm Back
If you thought you'd seen the last of me
* you're mistaken*
To go on with a show without me is like
* cabbage without bacon*

Or a whistle without a pea
Or a dog without a flea
'Cause you can't keep a good man down
* and to try is iniquitous*

167

'S Wonderful!

And you've no chance when you're dealing
*   with me, I'm ubiquitous*
I'm back to show you how it's done
I'm back, there was never really anyone else

Who could entertain you like you deserve
Few, if any others, would have the nerve
To face an audience like this
Whose ignorance is definitely bliss

But if you want a show there's only one place to go
Look on the night and where you see
*   my name in lights*
That's where you form a queue

Because I'm Back

Remember the photo of my sisters and brother in 1953?
Here we all are again, about to do what we love best – SING!
(From left: Maura, Ursula, Patricia, Kevin, Fionnuala, Phil,
Maeve and Michael)

And how right Billy was. Two days after my farewell party I was asked to go on air again with *Drivetime*. The programme was running a competition in which listeners were invited to write parody songs – did I think I could accompany them as they sang? Well, of course I did, at the drop of the highest hat! And that is how I went on. If anyone needed a singer or a piano player, I was ready, able and more than willing. Lord knows, I'd had plenty of practice.

Chapter 15

Faraway Places with Strange-Sounding Names

I love to travel. I got a taste for it when I organised that one-day trip to the Isle of Man for my family, and later when I took off on a tour of the United States followed by the trip to Kenya. But it was the wanderlust of my youngest sister Maeve that really got me going (you may remember my mother's poem that spoke of Maeve being possessed by the lure of foreign travel). Maeve went to Pakistan on a mission with the International Labour Organization in 1969. There she met her Danish husband Ejvind Mogensen, also working with the ILO, and together they travelled the world, with me in hot pursuit!

One of their most interesting postings was Antigua in the West Indies. They invited me out to see them in 1980. Noreen Nichol, my BA at the time, had recently had a car accident and injured her back. I thought the heat would be good for her bones so I asked her along. We loved the island and discovered there were 365 beaches, one for every day of the year. The night falls quickly in the tropics, and with the cover of darkness the insects emerge. Driving home one evening we were horrified by the sight of huge tarantulas scuttling along the dusty roads. During the day these spiders burrow into large holes that are all over the island; some people burn them out so they cannot bite their children. Maeve found a dead tarantula in her washing room beside the house. She could not bear to pick it up and asked the housekeeper to dispose of it. During her travels Maeve had seen enough un-savoury practices in relation to food to make her extremely careful in its preparation. She boiled everything first and then roasted it for hours in the oven to avoid tummy trouble. The one thing we did not have to fear in Antigua was a snake. Long ago someone introduced the mongoose to the island and that was the end of snakes.

Maeve, Ejvind, Noreen and myself went to the casino one night and I played a slot machine. Suddenly lights flashed and bells jangled and there was great excitement as money spilled into the dish in front of me. I had won the jackpot! My sensible sister dragged me away before I squandered the lot by piling it all back in the machine. The following night we went to an open-air movie at the army base, and it was so nice sipping beer and watching *Gone with the Wind.* Ah yes, tomorrow is another day.

And it was another day, some ten years later, when I re-visited Antigua with Cathal MacCabe. I wanted him to see Nelson's Dockyard in the English Harbour with its historic buildings and restaurants that serve the best red snapper in the world. Travelling with Cathal is a joy because he al-ways does his homework and plans his trips meticulously, but even his best efforts could not prevent the week begin-ning badly and almost ending in disaster. When we arrived in Antigua airport, we discovered that our luggage was on its way to Barbados. Cathal's heart tablets were in his bag, so I made a fuss. I should not have bothered. The lady at the desk shrugged and said there was nothing she could do; maybe it would turn up in a couple of days, maybe not. We had left a cold country wearing jumpers and overcoats, and here we were standing in the sweltering sun wondering what to do next. It was Kenya all over again. At our hotel the owner directed us to a shop where we could buy shorts, short-sleeved shirts and toiletries – evidently he was used to people arriving bagless. Cathal managed without his tablets, but we were mighty glad when the luggage did appear a day later.

We were at a bar on the beach one day when a guy shouted, 'Hey! Are you Kevin Hough?' He had been a manager in Jurys Hotel, Dublin and his mother was a huge fan of *The Lyrics Board*. As I said to Cathal, 'How come all my fans are mothers and grandmothers?' The guy then worked at a hotel on the island and he invited us over for dinner the next night.

Cathal and I put on our best light clothing and off we went in a taxi. We had a delicious meal and afterwards I was introduced to the piano. As I was playing, the glamorous crew from a British Airways flight came in (it was the hotel they used when they overnighted in Antigua) and we started a singsong that lasted until three in the morning. The next day the manager of the hotel phoned to ask if I would be interested in providing the entertainment over Christmas and the New Year, all expenses paid, including flights and accommodation, and a fee on top; he just had to clear it with his boss. I told him I would check my work schedule with RTÉ when I got back. As it happened, I could have taken leave, but after several phone calls and letters I could not get a proper deal, so decided to stay at home.

Another night Cathal and I went for dinner about a mile from our hotel. After our meal we ordered a taxi, but it took so long in coming that we decided to walk back because the road was well lit with a full moon. We had only gone a short way when a car passed us. It turned around and drove back towards us so I assumed it was our taxi. It stopped. Four guys got out. They flashed knives at us and demanded all our money. Cathal quickly secreted his credit cards down the front of his trousers and I threw a handful of coins on the ground. As they were picking up the coins, we ran like holy hell and hid behind some bushes. We discovered that Cathal had lost his cards, so we waited until the guys had driven off to go in search of them but could not find them. I put a branch at the side of the road to indicate where I should look, and at dawn the next day I went back but still no joy, so we cancelled them straight away. Luckily, my traveller's cheques got us by.

The next day we had lunch with friends of my sister who told us that things had become much more violent on the island since my first visit. There had recently been an incident when a couple of tourists had been threatened and guns put in their mouths. That was scary, so when the deal fell through with the hotel at Christmas, I was more relieved than disappointed. I had, however, met a very nice presenter at the local radio station and we did a link-up with her a few months after I got back.

When Maeve and Ejvind and their family were posted to the island of Trinidad, I went out to see them. There, too, were all kinds of insects, but they kept a large pet lizard in the house whose job was to gobble up any creepy crawly he came across. When there was no action, he lived behind a book-case. One night Maeve and Ejvind had to go to the school for a parents' meeting and I was left to babysit. A huge moth fluttered in the window and began making strange noises. The children were terrified, so I grabbed a can of insect spray and, intrepid hunter that I am (years of practice in the shop) I got him with one blast. The moth landed right beside the bookcase. Quick as a flash the lizard appeared, scooped up the moth and retreated. Next thing the lizard, guardian of the house, emerged into the room coughing and spluttering. I was convinced I had poisoned him and would have some explaining to do to my darling sister. I am pleased to say that he must have had a great constitution because he recovered, and I did not have to face the music.

One weekend we flew to the twin island of Tobago. It has lovely beaches but they can be quite dangerous. I am not a swimmer and did not venture far from the water's edge. I was playing there with my nieces when out of the blue a huge wave crashed down, turning us every which way and luckily throwing us up onto the sand. It was very frightening and a reminder of how, in the simplest circumstances, accidents can happen.

India is a country of such contrasts, some of them quite shocking. While there are many interesting things to see and do, I found the poverty upsetting because as an individual there is not much that you can do while you are there. At an outdoor food market in Delhi I saw swarms of flies guzzling on the raw meat and vegetables that were on display, which did not seem to deter local shoppers at all. Every time our car slowed down, hordes of children with all kinds of disabilities would chase after us begging for help. Despite the colours, the smells and extraordinary sights in the city, and the trip to Agra to see the Taj Mahal, I could not shake off my feeling of hopelessness at the immensity of the destitution, and in the end I was glad to leave.

However, sometimes you can do something. Once, when I was in The Gambia, a man selling carved wooden sculptures came up to me on a beach. He told me that he was trying to get the money to return to his wife in Senegal. I liked the look of one of his sculptures, a boat rowed by natives, but he had a big price on it. I knew I was supposed to haggle but I am not too good at it. In the end I thought I had done the guy a favour by paying over the odds, but when Maeve saw it she said I had got a bargain. As I travelled I collected a lot of holiday souvenirs, but invariably these things look different when you get them home, so most ended up in the charity shop, and I only have about three pieces left. I sometimes wonder if that sculptor ever did get back to Senegal.

I have been to some wacky restaurants in my time, many of them in Bangkok, which I visited when Maeve lived there. For my birthday one year, I took her family to a place called Cabbages and Condoms, where the owners contribute a percentage of their takings to support an AIDS project. When we arrived, the first thing we saw was a basket full of condoms, all free. They also had a condom store, which was a real curiosity shop with key rings containing condoms and gift items that were condom-related. The food is excellent and there is a good atmosphere in the building.

The Royal Dragon Restaurant is supposed to be one of the largest in the world. It has roller-skating waiters and waitresses. Our order was taken and the guy skated off to the kitchen. The next second someone else skated up with the wine list. The food and the wine were skated over to us in five minutes – I never saw anything so fast. Another restaurant we went to looked just like a supermarket with all the produce on display. We collected our baskets and selected uncooked meat and fish from the huge array on offer, and then we went to other counters to choose our vegetables. At the checkout we paid for our items and were shown to our table. The waiter came over, checked our baskets and asked how we wanted everything cooked, then brought our food to the kitchen. Twenty minutes later he was back with the prepared dishes. After dinner we selected desserts from another counter. Maeve was a bit dubious about the place because it was so open, and she had reservations about how the food was cleaned, prepared and cooked. She said she would not have been surprised if rats came in during the night and had a feast on the scraps.

Mind you, I played piano in Ta Sé Mahogany Gaspipes Restaurant in Dublin some years ago. On my first night there, when all the customers had gone, the owners invited me to take a glass of wine with them, which was very nice, but when they opened a door and let their Siamese cats loose on the tables it gave me quite a turn! That restaurant is now closed; I wonder why.

I have travelled a lot in Europe. Many years ago, my BA Jane Reid and I were working on *Poparama* and we went to Lisbon for a children's programmes conference. As we boarded the Aer Lingus flight, I was surprised to find that the senior hostess was a friend of mine, Phil Cassidy, and she upgraded us to first class. Other journalists were travelling on the same flight and it was priceless to see the looks on their faces as they passed us to go down the back – I am sure they thought I had a huge budget for the trip. In Lisbon we met a couple of guys from the BBC and hung around with them. The conference arena was arranged like a United Nations meeting that you would see on television. There were broadcasters and producers from different countries and our names were displayed in front of our microphones. When I was called on to speak about my programmes, an interpreter gave the translation on a microphone near me. I must have been nervous because at one stage she said I was talking too fast and asked me to slow down. In between meetings Jane and I had a lot of fun exploring the city and trying out the restaurants.

Ruth Buchanan and myself went to a similar conference in Vienna. We expected the same sort of set-up, but the entire proceedings were conducted in German. When I asked if we could be given a translation, we were told no, so there seemed little point in attending. I asked Ruth if she would like to return home or stay and enjoy a junket, and you can guess the answer to that one! We went to the opera to hear Placido Domingo, took tours around the city and visited the magnificent Schönbrunn Palace. Ruth was always a joy to be away with, whether in Ireland with *Poparama* or abroad. Before leaving Vienna, I did give one interview to a journalist from Austria who was impressed when he heard the range of our children's radio programmes that he said equalled if not bettered anything in Europe. Back at RTÉ I drew heavily from this conversation for my report to the Director General, and he seemed well satisfied.

One year I took off to Munich Beer Festival with a DJ friend. We stayed in a really cheap hotel. The dining room of the hotel was right beside our room so as the other guests were eating their breakfast, we were skipping down the hall to relieve ourselves in the nearest bathroom having spent the previous day drinking many tankards of beer. *Prost!* My friend is the best of company and ready to try anything, even a gigantic roller coaster, but as we turned upside down all the coins fell out of his pocket.

We had enough money left for a meal in an Italian restaurant. I went to the bathroom and I must have been a while because when I came back my buddy had fallen asleep into his spaghetti, and when I lifted his head his face looked like the rings on an electric cooker. We fell out of the place laughing. I found a supermarket trolley and put him into it to wheel him back to the hotel. We got to the main street but the footpath was very high, the trolley tipped over and he and I were thrown out on to the road. Luckily, nothing was coming or both us could have been seriously injured. So, as the song goes, we picked ourselves up, brushed ourselves down and eventually made it back. The next day, my friend brandished his new German phrase book in a restaurant and ordered a steak. This caused the waitress no end of amusement as she explained that what he had actually asked for was a babysitter!

There was another side to that visit. We went to visit the concentration camp at Dachau. It is the kind of place that cannot fail to make an impression. When we arrived, a coachload of American tourists had also just arrived and they made a rush for the gate as if it was just another castle or cathedral. One of the things I remember vividly is that, though there were trees all around the camp, the place was in complete silence with not a song from any bird. You can learn about these places and all the atrocities that went on but when you go there and see the gas ovens and the execution pits, it is another matter entirely. My friend was very upset by the whole experience. Later that night we met two

German soldiers and talked about our visit. They said they understood that foreigners would find it hard to forget and forgive the events of their terrible past, but modern Germans had to get on with living their lives in a country that was changed utterly from that of the past.

France was and is my favourite European country. For a number of years I travelled to Cherbourg with friends to buy wine. There were tastings first, of course, and my sister Phil's late husband John Lyons would amuse us by pretending to be a great connoisseur. He would sip the wine and declare in a pompous accent, 'This is a cheeky little wine and I am amused by it's impertinence.' We usually went in the spring and then again in the autumn and brought home about 30 cases, not all for myself I hasten to add. I took orders from relations and friends, and I always liked to have a few bottles in my shed when someone called and for special events.

One year eight of us went. My brother Michael had a friend who worked in the restaurant on the ship and he always made sure that we had a complimentary bottle with our dinner, and on the way back we would look after him with some of our loot. On this occasion, when we were leaving the ship we asked him what time it was departing. He gave us the Irish time and when we arrived back there was the ship, sailing out to sea. Panic set in. I had to be in RTÉ the next day. My nephew Félim Gormley had a gig, and my brother Michael was needed in his shop. The three of us thought about taking a train to Paris and flying home, leaving the cars with some of the other chaps to drive home. However, I noticed a cargo ship berthed nearby and I pleaded with them to take the eight of us. I must have had a really sad face because they took our cars, the booze and us on board,

*With Patricia – not catching hedgehogs this time,
but still having adventures together*

and then they fed us and got us all back to Dublin in time for our various commitments – brilliant! When I later explained to the ferry company that we had been misinformed about the departure time, they were good enough to send me a couple of vouchers.

It was during those trips that France grew on me as a country, so when Cathal phoned me in September 2002 to say he had found a very nice place to stay not too far from Perpignan we decided to go there for a week. It was a small village on the coast called Collioure, close to the Spanish border. We lived in style at a five-star hotel and every day we took bus trips into the surrounding countryside. It is just an enchanted area of France. I had been thinking of buying somewhere in the sun and it seemed like the perfect place.

On Wednesday I called into an estate agent in Collioure to enquire about properties that might be available, but she was completely disinterested. On Thursday we took the train to Port-Vendres, the village a bit further south. It is a fishing port with a beautiful little harbour surrounded by old houses and I fell for it at once. I immediately searched out an estate agent. Zorah had little or no English but she sent for her friend Geraldine, who did. They had three properties that they thought might suit. The first two were dark and old but the third was a dream. It was an apartment with a wonderful terrace and lots of plants and colourful pots. A German couple were selling it and there was a bit of haggling over the price but by Friday I had my apartment. The agency helped me find a solicitor and by the time I left on the Saturday, the documents were signed and the deal was done.

I was so excited to return to my own place on the coast the following year. It has been a wonderful retreat. I am not too good at the language but the people are very friendly and I now have many friends who live close by. Joan La Grue and her partner Jim Fahey have an apartment in Argelès-sur-Mer, and Ruth Buchanan and her husband Shane Ross have a house in Banyuls-sur-Mer. I love it when friends like Deirdre Purcell come to see me. We are the best of pals. I played the piano at her wedding to Kevin Healy and afterwards she took all the guests for a viewing of *Some Like it Hot* with Marilyn Monroe, my favourite movie star. She is one classy lady, and she certainly knows how to entertain. Deirdre celebrated her birthday in Port-Vendres a few years ago and friends arrived from all over for a terrific party. I now spend nine weeks of the year in Port-Vendres; it is where I have done almost all the writing for this book.

Chapter 16

A Spoonful of Sugar

I suppose we should expect some sort of illness as we get on in years. I thought I might have heart problems like my father, or cancer like my mother. During Mam's illness, my sister Fionnuala also got cancer, which was awful for her and our family. I am happy to say that, nearly forty years later, she is well and out walking her dog every day. After her operatic career, Fionnuala concentrated on painting, and has been successful in that, too. My grandmother and two of my aunts were not so fortunate; all died of the disease.

Now I would like to tell you a cautionary tale.

I began to feel unwell in 2014. My doctor sent me to hospital for blood tests. These revealed nothing untoward, so, despite not feeling the best, I carried on with my usual hectic schedule. I had agreed to direct *The Sound of Music* at the Briery Gap Theatre, and a couple of months later I was on the Cork train heading for rehearsals in Macroom when I received a phone call. My doctor said he had missed something when reading the test results, but there was no need to hurry back; he would sort it out on my return.

During rehearsals I became quite ill. A local doctor thought it was a chest infection and prescribed antibiotics. I stayed to see the show through, and was delighted for the cast, and especially for all the young people involved, that it was such a hit.

Back in Dublin, my GP arranged for more blood tests, which came back clear. By then I was experiencing back pain, and worried because of my family's medical history. I went to another clinic for tests, and was again informed that everything was normal. But everything was not normal. Several months later, it came to light that the initial test had revealed a paraprotein in my blood that could indicate a dangerous condition. My doctor booked me in for X-rays.

I had lunch with an old friend, Peter Mooney, one of RTÉ radio's truly great producers. I knew Peter was undergoing treatment for a blood disorder and the conversation naturally veered in that direction. When I mentioned my paraprotein result he said it looked as if it had been detected in time. Our meal ended on an optimistic note, but sadly, that was the last time I saw him. He passed away a few months later.

The X-rays threw no light on my condition, and I asked for a scan. I was told that scans are expensive and there is a waiting list, and besides I did not need one. Weeks went by, and more futile tests followed. I happened to be walking past the doctor's surgery one day when my pain was so severe that I had to go in.

My regular GP was busy, so I saw another doctor. She said physiotherapy might relieve the pain, and suggested the Milltown Clinic, near my house. It was fortunate that she did. A young physiotherapist detected something sinister at the back of my neck. At last – vindication! Straightaway, she sent me to hospital for further X-rays.

It was as my doctor was explaining the negative results from this last batch of X-rays that I finally blew up. 'I am not wasting your time,' I shouted. 'I am not well. When I cough the pain is piercing.'

An MRI scan was arranged for the following Wednesday at the Affidea Clinic in Dundrum, and on Friday I received a call from my doctor to say that we had a problem. All I could say was, 'I should have had that scan over a year ago.'

I was admitted into St Vincent's Hospital immediately. The consultant examined my charts closely and said, 'Kevin, this is extremely serious.' The scan had revealed a myeloma tumour close to my spine. Specialists were quickly assembled to discuss whether they should transfer me to the Mater Hospital for a risky ten-hour operation, or treat me with radiation. Considering the position of the tumour, they decided radiation was the best option.

They had to act immediately; the lower vertebrae in my spine could collapse at any time, causing paralysis. There is no weekend radiation facility in St Vincent's, so I was rushed by ambulance to St Luke's Hospital in Rathgar. As soon as I arrived, my consultant checked my legs, and was relieved that I still had movement. Treatment started at once, and only then could I reflect on how close I had come to never walking again. Two-and-a-half weeks of deep radiotherapy were followed by six months of chemotherapy.

I appreciate all the consultants and nursing staff at St Vincent's and St Luke's. Their swift reactions and superb care saved my mobility; perhaps even my life. And how can I ever thank the physiotherapist at the Milltown Clinic?

She took the time to listen to me, and then discovered an anomaly on my spine, which gave me the courage of my own convictions. But for her, well, I might never have finished this book.

I was in the public hospital for one week and then transferred to the private hospital for four weeks. Jimmy Magee, the sports commentator, was on my ward for a while, and we had such a laugh about the old days in Radio Éireann. I was weak and open to infection, so visitors were strictly limited. My sisters and brother were so supportive, and it was heartening to see close friends and many of my former assistants from RTÉ, if only for a short chat. Jane Reid, Sinead Renshaw and Helen Howard dropped by. Mark Shannon arrived with smoked salmon and brown bread, Frank Ryan sang a song or two, Cathal MacCabe and Ruth Buchanan came regularly. My myeloma is treatable but not curable at this point in time. I take a lot of medication. Physiotherapy is important and I do exercises every day. I can walk without a stick and am driving again. I remain positive that I will get rid of this cancer eventually.

So, the conclusion of my tale is: you know yourself and your body better than anybody. If you have a pain or an ailment, do not be fobbed off by anyone; you are the expert here. And remember, X-rays do not show up everything. Demand a scan!

When I look back on all the activities I have packed into my life – singing, dancing, acting, directing, producing, travelling, RTÉ, radio, television, stage; and on all the people who have loved and encouraged me to seize the golden opportunities that came along – I am filled with gratitude.

For my retirement party, Ruth wrote a song to the tune of 'Piano Man' and the chorus goes like this:

> *Sing us a song, you're the piano man,*
> *Sing us a song tonight.*
> *We're all in the mood for a melody,*
> *And you've got us feelin' all right.*

My life has been music, music all the way, and it has been *'S Wonderful! 'S Marvelous!*

Index

Index

191

Smith, Kathryn, 150
Sound of Music, The, 156, 182
St Dominic's Past Pupils' Union
    Drama Society, 57
St Louis Convent School, 21, 23
St Louis Infant School, 23, 24
St Louis Past Pupils' Musical
    Society, 23, 24
St Luke's Hospital, Rathgar, 184
St Mary's Junior School, 24, 33
St Vincent's Hospital, 184
Stella Cinema, Rathmines, 26
Student Prince, The, 26, 37
Studley, Eileen, 40, 41
Studley, Louise, 37, 40, 126, 127
Sunday Miscellany, 41, 78
Sunday Night at the Gaiety, 102
Sunday Night Play, 55

Ta Sé Mahogany Gaspipes, 176
Taylor Thompson, Trish, 81
Technical College in Rathmines,
    36
Telefís Éireann, 34, 77
Terenure College, 162
The Gambia, 23, 175
The Very Best of Broadway, 144
Theatre Nights, 114, 116–19, 121,
    123, 126, 127, 153, 160
Theatre Royal, 26, 60, 74
This is Your Half-Hour Call, 46
Thurles Musical Society, 97
Tina, 85
Tinker, Jack, 118
Tipperary Song Contest, 158
Tóibín, Niall, 123
Tomteland, Sweden, 83
Torsney, Joan, 82, 166
Tracey, Olivia, 131
Treston, Dan, 113
Trinidad and Tobago, 173, 174
Tubridy, Ryan, 81, 167
Tucker, Marie and Fergus, 34, 35
Tullamore Musical Society, 147

Tullamore Tribune Awards, 91
Twink, 23, 24, 111, 112, 129, 131,
    166, 167
Tynan, Kathleen, 123
Tynan, Ronan, 134, 136
Tynan, Rose, 137
Tyrrell, Maura, 22, 37, 38

Ustinov, Sir Peter, 118
Veronica Dunne Singing
    Competition, 130
Vicar Street, Dublin, 86
Vienna, Austria, 177

Waddell, Ginette, 55
Walsh, Ann, 132
Walsh, Ronnie, 78
Walshe, Catherine, 66
Waltzes from Vienna, 146
Ward, Tony, 129
Warren, Tommy, 47, 68, 79
Waterford International Festival
    of Music, 22, 23, 146
Watkins, Kathleen, 138
West Side Story, 71, 119, 121
Wheatley, Jo, 166
Whelan, Marty, 131
White, Alex, 132
Whitehall Road, Churchtown, 106
Whyte, Jacinta, 99, 104
Wilson Cup, 38
Winkless, Jackie, 133, 136
Wogan, Terry, 46, 78
Wolfe Tones, 96
Wolfe, Nyle, 134
Words and Music, 113, 114
Wylie, Liam, 111

Yeomen of the Guard, 39, 46
Yoplait Ireland, 86
Yoplait Song Contest, 86
Young, Simon, 81

Zig and Zag, 84